The Meeting

Charlotte Jones has written six previous stage plays:
Airswimming, *In Flame*, *Martha, Josie and the Chinese
Elvis*, *Humble Boy*, *The Dark* and *The Lightning Play*.
She won the Critics' Circle Most Promising Playwright
Award, 1999. *Martha, Josie and the Chinese Elvis* won
the Pearson TV Best New Play Award and Manchester
Evening News Best New Play Award, 1999. *Humble Boy*
won the Critics' Circle Best New Play, 2001, Susan Smith
Blackburn Award, People's Choice Best New Play, 2001,
and was nominated for an Olivier Award and a Drama
Desk Award. It ran at the National Theatre and in the
West End and has since been produced all over the world.
She wrote the book for Andrew Lloyd Webber's musical
of Wilkie Collins' novel *The Woman in White* (lyrics
by David Zippel) which ran in the West End and on
Broadway. She has also written extensively for TV, film
and radio.

by the same author

CHARLOTTE JONES

The Meeting

ff

FABER & FABER

First published in 2018
by Faber and Faber Ltd
74–77 Great Russell Street
London WC1B 3DA

Typeset by Country Setting, Kingsdown, Kent CT14 8ES
Printed in England by CPI Group (UK) Ltd, Croydon CR0 4YY

A CIP record for this book is available from the British Library

978–0–571–35050–6

2 4 6 8 10 9 7 5 3 1

The Meeting was first performed on the Minerva stage of the Chichester Festival Theatre on 13 July 2018. The cast was as follows:

Rachel Lydia Leonard
Adam Gerald Kyd
Alice Jean St Clair
Tabitha Leona Allen
Biddy Olivia Darnley
Nathaniel Burns Laurie Davidson
James Rickman Jim Findley

Director Natalie Abrahami
Designer Vicki Mortimer
Lighting Designers Paule Constable and Marc Williams
Music and Sound Ben and Max Ringham
Choreographer Mark Smith
Movement Director Gary Sefton
Casting Director Charlotte Sutton

Characters

Alice Thirley
sixties, deaf

Rachel Young
thirties, hearing, fluent in sign language

Adam Young
forties

Biddy Rickman
thirties

James Rickman
fifties

Tabitha Rickman
sixteen

Nathaniel Burns
early twenties

THE MEETING

Our life is love, and peace, and tenderness;
and bearing one with another, and forgiving
one another, and not laying accusations
one against another; but praying one
for another, and helping one another up
with a tender hand.

Isaac Penington, 1667

Act One

*1805. The Meeting Place. A circle. Spring. Chalky soil
and stones.*

*The members of the Meeting for Worship are gathered.
Adam Young is a strong, quiet man in his forties. Rachel,
his wife, is vibrant with an unconventional beauty, thirties.
Alice Thirley is Rachel's mother – late fifties, early sixties,
piercing. She is deaf. James Rickman is the elder today,
late fifties, cerebral, earnest, and with him, his wife Biddy,
plump, attractive, late thirties, and his daughter Tabitha,
sixteen, pert, pretty. There are perhaps five more members
of the Meeting gathered. This is a largely ageing population.*

*They do not speak. After a period of silence Rickman
stands.*

Rickman Friends, I must warn you that tonight there will
be rejoicing in the town. There has been a victory for the
troops and the town will, as a consequence, be illuminated.
No doubt there will be drinking and debauchery. Our
presence there would be seen as a provocation. For the
time being therefore I would urge that we keep to
ourselves. There will be no rejoicing in our hearts over
the destruction of our fellow men. Let them break our
windows. Let them slander us. We will remain true to
ourselves. We will not place our dependence on fleets and
armies, but we will be peaceful in ourselves, in our words
and our actions. In the words of our dear founder: 'We
utterly deny all outward wars and strife and fightings
with outward weapons, for any end and under any
pretence whatsoever. And this is our testimony to the
whole world.' I give thanks for our declaration to peace
and that we can live here together in harmony. Let us, in

this time of war, be an example to our fellow men of the true path of no violence.

He sits. His ministry settles. Then he turns to the man on his right – Adam – shakes his hand. The others shake hands. The Meeting disperses. Only Alice remains.

SCENE TWO

Rachel and Adam's house. Spring.
Alice goes to a large wooden blanket-box and takes out her sewing. She sits and sews.
Rachel enters and watches her mother. Alice stretches her hands out – the sewing is causing her strain these days. Rachel goes up and taps her lightly on the shoulder. Alice doesn't look round but smiles – knows her daughter's touch, holds her hand a moment. They both sign.

Rachel *Your Hands? Tired?*

Alice shakes her head.

Alice *My hands are strong.*

Rachel *No more sewing.*

Rachel tries to take away her sewing.

Alice *You were a long time.*

Rachel *I walked.*

Alice *Sad?*

Rachel shakes her head, smiles. She speaks.

Rachel No, not sad –

Then she signs:
Happy! Full of life.

4

Alice touches Rachel's face.

Mamma.

>*Rachel puts out her hands. Alice surrenders her hands to her and relaxes as Rachel massages them. Adam enters. Looks at them.*

Adam Do her hands trouble her still?

>*Alice doesn't hear him, of course. Rachel stirs her, indicates to her that Adam is back.*

Rachel It's all the sewing.

>*Adam signs chattering hands. He's in a teasing mode.*

Adam And all the talking. Mother and daughter – all day – behind my back.

Rachel (*teasing him back*) Do you feel excluded, husband?

Adam From your woman talk? I have my mind on higher things.

Rachel You are a true Quaker, Adam!

>*Alice nudges her daughter, wants to be included.*

Adam wants to talk with his hands.

>*Alice smiles – this is a great joke between them.*

Alice *You and me? We can talk. All night.*

Adam (*smiling*) What did she say?

Rachel She wants to talk with you, Adam. All night long.

Adam Tell her I need my sleep.

Rachel *He's scared of you, Mamma.*

>*Alice chuckles.*

Alice (*to Adam*) *Eat?*

Adam (*nodding, echoing her 'eat' sign*) Yes. Let's eat. You're good to me, Alice.

Alice smiles, pinches Adam's cheek, exits to get their food. Adam takes Rachel in his arms, kisses her neck. After a moment, Rachel shakes him off, laughs, looks at her dress. It's covered in chalk. She pats her dress, mock-annoyed.

Rachel Your hands are full of chalk!

Adam It is God's own chalk.

Rachel You find your every excuse in God.

Adam Where else?

He touches her. She pushes him away lightly.

Rachel (*laughing*) Cleanliness before godliness, Adam.

He holds her more strongly.

Adam I need to talk to you.

Rachel Ah! Now he wants to talk.

Adam You are different today. You are happy! Are you?

Rachel I saw my first swallow today. Summer is coming.

Adam (*concerned*) You went walking?

She pulls away from him. She goes to fetch a pitcher of water for him to wash his hands.

Rachel Not far.

Adam Did you keep from the town?

Pause.

Rachel I held God in my head, as you told me.

Adam It is not safe for you. A woman alone. Did you not hear what James said? The talk in the town is only of the wars.

Rachel And the hero dead. I saw a mother today – weeping for her dead son. I spoke to her –

Adam Why will you not listen to me?

Rachel I wanted to comfort her. Do we not have a ministry to help those who suffer?

Adam We are not welcome in the town at this time –

Rachel Her son was sixteen years old. A child still.

Adam What did you say to her?

Rachel I told her of our testimony. She laughed at me and told me her younger son wants to enlist too. That she would lose him too rather than be like me!

Adam She knows no better.

Rachel A man came up to me then and told me to go. He said her son was a hero. That we must all celebrate his death. That anyone who did not was a traitor.

Adam You left then I hope?

Rachel (*nods*) But Adam, our testimony to peace meant nothing to them. They glory in war. They seem to find their identity in it. We are an irrelevance to them. What good are we if we sit here in silence and watch as the world burns?

Adam We lead by example.

Rachel But how can we if no one looks in our direction?

Adam washes his hands.

Adam You must not go to the town any more. Give me your word.

Rachel You know I like to walk, Adam. It clears my head.

Adam You can walk elsewhere.

Rachel You go to the town!

Adam For my work only.

Rachel How comes it, that I cannot talk to the townspeople but you can commemorate their dead?

Pause.

Adam That is different. We have always traded in the town.

Rachel Perhaps you will be the one to carve the stone for that child. An empty grave for a lost soldier boy. Maybe your words will glorify his dying. Your words will make a hero of him.

Adam I am a stonemason. I must make tombstones.

Rachel But these are not Quaker dead.

Adam (*rattled*) We hold all in the light. All men equal. Alive or dead. Besides I do not choose the words . . . What would you have me do? Gravestones must still be carved . . .

Rachel Does peace not start in the words we think and speak – the words we write?

Adam I have squared myself with it.

Rachel If you bury their hero dead, it may be said that you make profit from these wars –

Adam Why must you always question like this?

Rachel I worry for your peace of mind. What do the elders say about it? Have you spoken to James?

Adam He is not my judge.

Rachel No. But he is your friend.

Adam If it will please you, I will talk to him.

Rachel smiles.

Rachel Thank you . . . What is it you wanted to tell me, husband?

She finds Adam a cloth and gives it to him. He wipes his hands. Alice re-enters with food. She prepares the table. Alice takes no notice of them at first but gradually she picks up on Rachel's discomfort.

Adam I need help. With my work.

Rachel looks at him.

Rachel What?

Adam With the inscription work. My eyes will not see them right. The letters fly about. If I mark the name wrong then I must cut a new stone. Last month I lost work. Lost money.

Rachel I can help you with the words.

Adam I thought you took exception to the words –

Rachel But I would like to be of use to you –

Adam I need a pupil. An apprentice. A boy.

Pause.

I must have someone who can read and write.

Rachel A Friend?

Adam A Friend of course. But there are no young boys suitable amongst us . . .

Rachel (*painfully*) No.

Adam I will enquire perhaps at Regional Meeting.

Rachel Will he live here?

Adam Where else?

Rachel In our house?

Adam He need not be strong. I can do the strength work. I can teach him. I am a master mason now. I know my trade. I have worked hard.

Rachel An apprenticeship? He would live here for seven years? In our house?

Adam There is room enough for the boy.

Rachel And what am I to him? What will I be?

Adam He would be – my apprentice. Nothing more. A business arrangement.

He glances at her – he knew this would upset her. Rachel says nothing. Adam sits at the table.

Alice *Eat?*

Rachel shakes her head.

Look at me. What is it?

Rachel *Nothing.*

Alice *Talk to me . . . You're troubled.*

Rachel *I'll tell you later.*

Alice *What did he say?*

Adam Stop it! Both of you. Please.

They both stop signing.

Rachel. Sit. We will say grace.

Rachel sits. Adam puts his hands together. Rachel's hands are restless. She fingerspells a name to herself.

Rachel *Nathaniel.*

Adam Be still your hands.

Rachel I'm thinking.

Adam Please. Don't spoil our good silence with your thoughts. Let us pray.

Alice quietens Rachel's hands, shakes her head at her, no. Rachel then puts her hands together and bows her head. Their grace is silent. Alice doesn't pray. She watches the other two. Adam finishes, looks up – smiles.

I am hungry, Good Alice. Let's eat.

Alice looks at him and then breaks the bread, hands it out. They start to eat in silence.

SCENE THREE

Adam exits. Biddy enters with her daughter Tabitha who holds the baby 'Mary' in her arms. A bundle of swaddled linen to represent the baby.

Biddy It does my soul good to see you, Friend.

Rachel Biddy. Tabitha. And little Mary. Look at her! How are your nights, Biddy?

Biddy Sleep is for the wicked. Of course the troubles we live with daily do not help. Did you hear they broke the windows of old Sam Grover's house last night? And then they flung dirt in his good wife's face!

Rachel Oh no! Our independence is seen as a threat. But we must continue to walk courageously over the world.

Alice gets a half-made quilt out of the linen box and a small box of linen squares and needles etc. This is their weekly quilting circle.

Biddy All I know is my nerves are shred.

Tabitha *(interrupting)* She won't settle, Mamma.

Biddy I have work to do –

Rachel I can hold the baby.

Biddy ignores this.

Biddy *(to Tabitha)* You want to play outside with the other children? Give the baby to me.

Tabitha hands the baby to her mother and runs off to play.

Rachel *(watching Tabitha)* I could feast my eyes on her all day. She's a rare lily.

Biddy One day she may be a match for you.

Rachel Biddy!

Biddy Is it a sin now to make a compliment?

Rachel No, but it's a sin to receive one.

Biddy That places us in a bind! Luckily we Quakers have no truck with sinning!

They smile. Alice hands Rachel a needle and thread and some squares of fabric. They start to 'quilt'.

She is after me to curl her hair – I am not against it – she would still wear plain dress – but her father won't hear of it –

Rachel There is no need to paint the lily.

Biddy She troubles her father.

Rachel He won't be the last man she troubles.

Biddy If we can find her a man – a Quaker –

Rachel She is so young, Biddy – there is time enough –

Biddy At least our men are not dying for King and Country. We have that advantage over the others. Our men have laid down their arms so they can protect us and plant their seed in us. Hah hah! We are not stupid. I told my Tabitha she will profit in many ways from our testimony to peace!

Rachel I don't think the early Friends had Tabitha in mind when they made the declaration.

Biddy No, no, no. But do not peace and harmony begin in the home? In the love between a husband and wife, a mother and her child?

Rachel (*quietly*) Indeed.

The baby grizzles.

Biddy Why will you not sleep, child?

Rachel puts out her hands.

Rachel Would you let me try?

Biddy I know little Mary would sleep if I could only sing to her. But my husband won't admit it – mindful of his duties – not even the whiff of a psalm! All night I must hear her cry.

Rachel If he is asleep, I think you might sing.

Biddy Oh, I do sing. But when I am least aware. I find I cannot help myself – sometimes the songs burst forth from me – in my sleep even.

Rachel As long as it's not during Meeting for Worship I see no harm.

Biddy That's the sorrow, dear Rachel. Sometimes in worship I sit in the silence and I can feel a tune rising up in me. I think – I am going to sing – so help me God – I cannot contain it. And not sacred tunes! Oh no.

Lewdness comes to me in the silence, dear Rachel, bawdy songs with improper melodies.

Rachel laughs.

Rachel Adam tells me I must try not to minister so often. In Meeting. That it is improper, there is a vanity in it.

Biddy Adam is a man of eminent piety.

Rachel But women have as much right to speak –

Biddy Indeed. We are fortunate daughters of the light – women as equal as their menfolk –

Rachel And yet in many Meetings they still keep us separate.

Biddy Not in our Meeting!

Rachel No. But it still seems that – not all truth has – equal weight . . . You never speak, Biddy. In Meeting. I have never once heard you minister.

Biddy I have enough to say outside of Meeting! I could not punish you all with more of my talk!

Rachel How do you do it? Keep silent.

Biddy I relish the silence . . . It is the incessant demands of my children make me desirous of it.

Pause.

Of course you are not a Quaker by birthright – only by convincement – it was dear Adam who led you and your mother to the light. Perforce the silence will come harder for you.

Rachel Adam says it is in the silence that we find God. But sometimes I fear it, Biddy. I fear what my thoughts will do to me in the silence. Sometimes I feel so stirred to words. To action.

Biddy You are too clever, Friend. It were best you had no thoughts in your head like me . . .

Rachel smiles.

Here, take little Mary for me. I grow weary.

Rachel takes the baby. Biddy stretches and then takes the sewing up.

Rachel Adam wants an apprentice.

Biddy That will be good for him. He has worked hard.

Rachel He does not want an apprentice, Biddy. He wants a son.

Biddy tuts, this is not so.

He has buried three boys. Carved their names. One by one. Nathaniel. And Nathaniel. And Nathaniel.

Biddy Rachel –

Rachel Not one breath among them. Not one moment of living – not one boy who could claim the name and live –

Biddy Step out of the darkness, Friend.

Pause. Rachel touches the blanket-box.

Rachel This box was my very first cradle you know – the box my Mamma laid me in when I was first born. She slept beside it on the floor – with a red ribbon tied 'twixt her wrist and mine – so she would know when I was crying. If I so much as stirred, the ribbon would pull her awake.

She looks to Alice. Alice is watching her.

My cradle, Mamma.

Alice smiles.

I want to wake to a cry – to a tug to my heart –

Biddy (*indicating the baby*) Let's try and lay her down, shall we?

She puts her hands out for the baby.

Let me take her.

Rachel Forgive me –

Biddy Shhh. She sleeps.

She looks around. Where to put the baby? Alice anticipates the action and makes a nest of blankets for the sleeping child.

Thank you, Good Alice.

She goes and lays the baby down. Alice smiles at the baby.

(*To Rachel.*) Have you been walking again?

Rachel I try to walk the thoughts away – just yesterday I felt better – I felt a lifting in me –

Biddy I wish I could walk with you. But these are unsettled times.

Alice goes and shakes out her large piece of quilt. She senses that Rachel is ill at ease.

Where do you go? To the town?

Rachel It matters not – I go anywhere and everywhere but I stay in the same place –

Biddy You must stop this, Rachel –

Rachel My womb is stone –

She signs it, inadvertently. Her first language.

Womb. Stone.

Alice *No. I had you. My miracle. You will too.*

Rachel shakes her head. Not convinced.

Rachel I am still young but I feel as if my life is over –

Biddy These thoughts are the devil's work –

Rachel Adam saved Mamma and me. Who else would have taken us in? A deaf woman and her girl. And I have given him nothing in return.

Biddy He loves you. Do you not know that?

Rachel I have failed him.

Biddy You are the rare flower amongst us, Rachel. He prizes you above all else – after God of course.

Rachel What shall I do, Biddy? Tell me.

Pause.

Biddy You must welcome a stranger into your home. Give Adam his apprentice.

Rachel In my heart I feel it is not right. A boy in my house. A boy where our son should be.

Biddy Cherish this boy. For Friend Adam's sake.

Silence. Rachel looks at the baby. Alice watches her.

Rachel She is lovely when she sleeps.

Biddy My children must be a rebuke to you – four healthy children –

Rachel You owe me nothing.

Biddy I am heartsick for you, Friend – I wish I could give her to you –

Rachel Biddy, don't say it, please! Give me a double portion of thy good spirit – that is all I want.

Rachel kisses Biddy, leaves. Biddy touches her baby.

She sings absently, quietly, a lullaby.

Biddy Let me see thy countenance,
Let me hear thy voice,
For sweet, oh sweet, is thy dear voice
And thy face is lovely, dear love.

SCENE FOUR

Biddy picks up her child and leaves. Alice leaves.
The Place of Stones. Near the sea. A young man enters:
Nathaniel Burns. He is beautiful, fit with an edgy quality,
early twenties. He's dressed in military gear – a brilliantly
coloured military jacket – although his jacket is undone
and he looks unshaven . . . He takes out a small knife
and an apple, cuts it with precision, eats and watches as
Rachel enters. She is carrying a basket of provisions. She
does not see him. She pauses on her journey. Nathaniel
watches her from behind. She kneels a moment before
three small stones. Gravestones. She reads what's written
there. Then she picks up a stone from nearby and looks
at it and puts it in her pocket. She gets up.

Nathaniel What are you doing?

She spins round, scared. Sees the knife.

Rachel Please – I am just walking.

Nathaniel What do you have in your basket?

Rachel Food. Are you hungry? Take it. I do not need it.
I am going home.

Nathaniel You were walking the other way. Towards the
town.

Rachel Do you mean me harm?

Nathaniel Why would I mean you harm?

18

Rachel You carry a weapon.

He throws away his apple. Takes a step closer. She steps back.

I was taking food to the town. For those who mourn.

He looks in the basket – takes out bread. He eats it hungrily.

Nathaniel You do not live in the town?

She shakes her head.

Rachel We live apart. We mean no harm to you – to anyone –

Nathaniel You are frightened!

Rachel No. It is just – the sight of your uniform – I am not accustomed –

Nathaniel You are right to be scared. I am trained to kill.

Rachel You must do what you see fit, Friend – kill me if you must – but I will endeavour to love you anyway.

Nathaniel looks at her and then he laughs. He puts the knife away carefully in his jacket pocket.

Why do you laugh?

Nathaniel I did not know I was your friend. We even now made acquaintance.

Rachel All men are my Friends.

Nathaniel You must keep yourself busy.

Rachel You misunderstand me. I am a member of the Society of Friends.

Pause.

Nathaniel I've heard of you. You quake before God, do you not?

Rachel Those who deride us have said so. Though – the Spirit rising inside – moving you to speak – can make you tremulous.

Nathaniel So you do not like my uniform? Most women do love the sight of it.

Rachel We do not take up arms. We cannot condone the destruction of any of God's creatures. Therefore we must mourn the dead on all sides.

Nathaniel You must be practised at mourning.

Rachel I am.

She looks at him.

We are small in number now – our members grow old – if we live quietly the militia do not press us.

Nathaniel (*interested*) Is that so? There is a skill to laying low especially in these turbulent times . . . What else do you believe?

Rachel We treat all alike – we speak the same 'you' to all. We do not believe in rank. We do not live by the world's salutations or fashions or customs. We do not pay tithes. We answer to that of God in every man. We are honest and speak plain – why do you smile?

Nathaniel I see I have arrived by chance in heaven.

Rachel You mock me. We live by our conscience. That is all. We do not conform to the multitude. We choose to be awake and not to accept the old ways of being. And that is radical in these times. But I must not delay you –

Nathaniel You do not delay me. I have nowhere to go.

Rachel What about your regiment?

Pause.

Nathaniel I have been invalided out.

20

Rachel So you will fight no more? That is good. But I see no injury on you.

Nathaniel Not all injuries are visible.

Pause.

Rachel My husband is waiting for me. Today we have Meeting for Worship – I should not be here.

Nathaniel Why did you put a stone in your pocket? When you arrived – I saw you –

Rachel takes the stone out of her pocket.

Rachel A silly game of mine. I am always looking for the perfect stone.

Nathaniel Are not all stones equal under God?

She smiles.

Rachel It is the perfect stone for me. For another person it might be an ordinary stone – with absolutely nothing to recommend it. This one would be too small for your hand – see. In fact this is not the right stone for me either.

She discards it. Looks again.

Mine must be white. And a perfect 'O'. It must fit in my palm. So I can turn it over and over. With my finger like this.

She demonstrates.

Nathaniel A fretting stone?

Rachel You could call it that. This one is a good shape. But too grey.

She discards it.

Nathaniel Small and white and round? I wager I can find it.

He starts to look. She watches him. He picks one up, shows it to her.

Here is one for me.

Rachel But it has a hole in it.

Nathaniel Perfect. Now you see through me.

A moment of connection.

Rachel Where will you sleep tonight?

Nathaniel Under the cover of the stars.

Rachel But what of your family – ?

Nathaniel Dead to me. I thought I would find refuge in the wars. Brotherhood at the very least. But I found only misery. And pain.

Rachel I am sorry for you . . . What is your name?

Nathaniel Nathaniel.

Rachel What?

He stands up, looks at her.

Nathaniel Nathaniel.

She is shocked. She shakes her head slightly.

Nathaniel Burns.

Rachel It is God's will.

Nathaniel What?

Rachel Can you read? Write?

Nathaniel Yes –

Rachel Then you must come with me.

Nathaniel What are you saying?

Rachel You must stay here with us. My husband and me. I can find you employment.

Nathaniel But I must keep moving –

Rachel We will keep you safe. We live apart – in these times of war it is our only choice. You can shelter with us – sleep once more in a bed. You can – recover yourself.

Nathaniel Are you in earnest?

She nods.

I would like work. Good, honest work.

Rachel (*hesitant*) But take off your coat. I think it were better we do not breathe a word of the militia. My husband would find it harder to accept you. I fear he might be disowned – or disciplined – for employing a military man. His membership is everything to him. We must say you are a Friend. Yes! One of us.

He takes off his jacket.

Nathaniel I can be one of you. Look, I quake already.

He holds up his hand – it shakes.

Rachel Do not mock me.

Nathaniel I do not. My hand is always thus. A souvenir from the battlefield . . . I have nightmares too.

Rachel Poor boy. I will help you.

Nathaniel I am in your debt.

Rachel We go to Meeting for Worship today. You must not betray yourself. Our Meeting for worship is in silence. There is no outward show – no priest – no noise of bells. You can be moved to speak – by the Spirit – but silence is revered by our elders.

Nathaniel But I do not believe in your God.

Rachel No matter . . . I will teach you how to be – in Meeting. At home. At all times – I will teach you. We will keep it as our secret. You and me.

She stops, looks at him.

I am Rachel. Come. I will tell you all.

She takes his jacket. They exit.

SCENE FIVE

Rachel and Adam's house.
Rachel enters with Nathaniel. She goes to the blanket-box. She places his jacket inside. Conceals it. She is excited, scared.

Rachel Adam? Adam!

The room's empty.

(*To Nathaniel.*) Wait here. I will find him.

After a few moments Alice enters like a spectre and stands behind Nathaniel, her face impassive. He suddenly becomes aware of her.

Nathaniel Forgive me. You surprised me.

She stares at him.

How do you do?

She stares at him.

I am Nathaniel Burns.

She stares at him.

I am the apprentice.

She stares at him.

Rachel brought me here. Mrs Young. I am come to live here. I am from the North. A Quaker. From the North. Do you live here?

Rachel re-enters.

Rachel Adam is coming to meet you. He is pleased. Ah! You have met my mother. Alice.

Nathaniel (*to Rachel*) She has a disarming way of regarding me.

Rachel laughs.

Rachel She is deaf! Forgive me, I should have told you. My mother never speaks. You must follow my mother at Meeting. Not me. The elders hold her in high regard.

Nathaniel Does she not understand you?

Rachel Not when I speak fast.

I tell him you are the elders' favourite.

Alice *Because I never speak!*

Rachel She reads hands. Lips are harder for her.

Alice is staring hostilely at Nathaniel.

Be nice to him.

Alice *Who is he?*

Rachel (*signs and speaks*) **He is Adam's apprentice.**

She stares at Nathaniel again.

Nathaniel I don't think she likes me.

Rachel She does. This is her way.

Alice *What is his name?*

Nathaniel What's she saying?

Rachel She wants to know your name.

Nathaniel Nathaniel.

Alice frowns – looks to her daughter for confirmation. Rachel signs. Rachel makes her home sign for Nathaniel. It speaks of a baby and loss.

Rachel *Shake his hand, Mamma?*

Alice repeats the sign for Nathaniel.

Alice (*shocked*) *Nathaniel? Nathaniel? No. This is all wrong. Send him away.*

Rachel *No, Mamma. God sent him. God gave him to me.*

Pause.

Nathaniel Pleased to meet you, Alice.

He puts out his hand to her. She won't shake it. Adam enters. Rachel jumps.

Rachel Adam!

Adam looks at Nathaniel.

(*Nervous.*) Adam. This is Nathaniel Burns.

Nathaniel (*using the wrong form of address*) Mr Young, I am indebted to you.

Nathaniel bows his head.

Adam (to Rachel) You said he was a Quaker.

Rachel (*worried*) There is no need to bow your head, Nathaniel. My husband's name is Adam.

Nathaniel Forgive me. I am nervous. I forgot myself.

Adam Where did you find him? In the town?

Rachel No – I did not go to the town –

Nathaniel We met by the roadside. I was walking.

Adam Where were you going?

Rachel He was going to the coast.

Adam You have family there?

Nathaniel looks at Rachel.

Rachel No, his family are in the North. Quakers from the North.

Adam What trade does your father follow?

Nathaniel My father is – a bookseller.

Adam You can read then?

Nathaniel And write, yes.

Adam That is a blessing.

Nathaniel I am the second son. My mother died recently. I held her in a dear light. I could not stay in the house without my mother. I felt a strong urge to travel. I needed to find myself once more. It is with my father's blessing that I set off.

Alice regards him coolly and turns and exits. Rachel ignores this.

Rachel Did you not pray for an apprentice, Adam?

Adam I cannot promise you anything –

Nathaniel No, sir –

Adam Why do you call me 'sir'? You must call me Adam. You are sure you are a member of our Society?

Nathaniel nods.

Rachel Being on the road has made him forget.

Adam looks at him.

Adam I must talk with the elders.

Nathaniel I feel a calling to good, honest work.

Rachel Is he not what you hoped for, Adam?

Adam It is hard work. Back-breaking work. We shall treat all as temporary till I am satisfied. Till then you may live with us in unity.

He regards Nathaniel coolly.

It is time for worship.

He turns round and leaves. Nathaniel smiles conspiratorially at Rachel. She looks down. Follows Adam. Nathaniel follows them both.

SCENE SIX

The Meeting. Rickman enters. Biddy hurries along behind him. She carries the baby. Tabitha follows. The Friends enter – they shake the Elder's hands and sit in the Meeting Place. A circle. Alice enters.

Rickman Alice. It does my soul good to see you!

Alice *I hold you in the light.*

Pause.

Rickman Quite! Quite!

Alice looks at him disdainfully.

Biddy Good Alice.

Tabitha Good Alice.

Adam enters, arm-in-arm with Rachel. Followed by Nathaniel.

Rickman Adam.

They shake hands.

Friend Rachel.

Adam This is Nathaniel Burns, James. He is come to be my apprentice.

Nathaniel smiles and follows Rachel and Adam into Meeting. Rickman and Biddy exchange looks of surprise. Tabitha smiles at Nathaniel. They follow them into Meeting.

Rachel indicates a place for Nathaniel to sit, where she can keep him in her eyeline. All the members of the Meeting take their chairs and sit in a circle. Rickman sits last. Bows his head. The silence begins. Nathaniel takes everything in. Alice never closes her eyes but witnesses everything.

Silence. A little shuffling. Tabitha is playing with her hair, bored. Eyes open. Closed again. Silence. Suddenly Rachel stands.

Adam (*quietly*) Rachel, forbear.

Rachel looks at her husband. She sits. Closes her eyes. But she cannot help it. She stands again. The words tumble out of her.

Rachel Friends, forgive me – I try to resist the Spirit – I do – but I find I am called once more to minister . . . This nation is again at war. They call this a just war. They tell us that we must fight the good fight against tyranny and evil. And the good citizens need no convincing because they fear anyone who is different – and the enemy surely deserves to die. Is not every war based on lies like this! . . . And here we sit contentedly with our testimonies to peace and truth and equality. But of what use are these testimonies when people are already dying? I met a woman this week. A mother weeping for her dead son. How do we comfort her? I fear that sitting in the silence is not enough. God forgive me, but prayer is not enough. I feel an obligation upon me – upon all of us – to take our message into the world. To go and stand on the front line if necessary. We must answer the violence – not with silence but with words and action! Now is not the time to *sleep*! Now is the time to *speak*! Truly I would not have a single one of us harmed – I know it is more dangerous for the men to venture forth. That is why we women, we wives and sisters must act. Is it not the woman's voice that is silenced in time of war? I believe that it is the duty of us as women to heal the world –

Biddy shakes her head, exchanges looks with her husband. Whispers something to Tabitha. 'Don't listen to her.' There is some discomfort in the Meeting.

Forgive me, Friends, if I trouble you. But let this silence that we cherish be a place where we can question ourselves fully – let it not be simply a false refuge from the troubles of the world –

There are shufflings among the assembled. Disquiet. 'What is she saying?' 'Why does she provoke us like this?'

Let us not live in fear – but rather take heed to the promptings of love and truth in our hearts!

More disquiet.

Alice *What are you saying? Why are they so disturbed?*

Rickman stands to 'elder' the Meeting. A very unusual occurrence. He looks at Alice. At all of them.

Rickman Friends. Must I remind you that this is ministry and must be met with silence?

Alice *You should listen to her. My daughter speaks with the tongue of the deaf.*

Rickman looks at her, disquieted but unable to understand her.

30

Rickman Centre down – please! We must let the – ministry – settle in us before we respond.

He looks at them and then he resumes his seat. They all try to bow their heads again – all except Nathaniel, who stares at Rachel. She looks up at him. A moment of connection between them. A few moments of silence. Then Rickman turns to Nathaniel, who is sitting beside him to shake his hand. Nathaniel stares at him uncomprehendingly for a moment and then remembers himself. All of them turn and shake hands: this signals the end of the Meeting.

Biddy Well. What an eventful Meeting!

Adam stands up quickly, goes to go. Rachel and Alice follow. Rickman stops Adam.

Rickman Adam. A word.

Rachel looks at him. Adam nods for her to go. She leaves with Alice. Rachel turns for Nathaniel to follow them. The Friends disperse.

Bedelia, leave us.

Biddy leaves reluctantly.

Biddy Come along, Tabitha. Let us see if we can meet our new Friend from the North!

Rickman and Adam are left.

Rickman May I speak plain? . . . I am worried about Rachel.

Adam I thought she spoke truth today. Perhaps we do grow introspective. Perhaps we become lazy in our resistance.

Rickman (*gently, concerned*) Perhaps yes. But with regard to Rachel – I fear the balance of her mind is disturbed. Her grief has led her to this. More's the pity. Her words are all emotion – they are impetuous, they fly forth from her mouth without due consideration –

Adam She was born into her mother's silence – sometimes she feels propelled into speech –

Rickman But this is not true ministry. It has the wrong source. She does not surrender fully to the silence, she does not listen for God, she does not refer to the Bible – there is no discernment, Adam –

Adam Do we not encourage ministry from our womenfolk? I fear you take objection to her words because she is a woman –

Rickman No, no, no. Do not mistake me, Adam, I welcome female ministry – Rachel has as much right to speak as any man – but she speaks too often – you know this is not our way – and furthermore she begins to disturb our members in both her words and her actions . . . I take it she is still venturing forth to the town?

Adam No. She gave me her word –

Rickman But this woman she spoke of? She is endangering herself. The town will take no heed of a young woman like Rachel. The townsfolk are not as enlightened as we are. For her to go forth to the town and to minister there – were to risk death –

Adam doesn't speak.

Rachel came from the world and I fear she is drawn back to the world.

Adam She speaks from her experience. She questions, she seeks for answers, only this.

Rickman Rachel's speaking is not ministry – it is protest, it is agitation. I feel we must find ways to help her, to ease

32

her restless spirit. As we both know, being an elder accords me no authority over this Meeting – I am an attentive listener to the needs of our Meeting, that is all – so I say this also as your friend, Adam. I am concerned for your wife's spiritual welfare and for yours too . . . I would not have her lead you towards the world.

Adam But should we stand so apart from the world?

Rickman We do not! I am answerable to London Yearly Meeting. I must follow their advices, answer to their queries – I must record all that happens here to Monthly Meeting. Everything we do here is held to account . . . But these are difficult times for us. We are not cherished by our fellow men. You know that. Things could get worse for us here, Adam.

Adam Yes.

Pause.

Rickman Who is this boy? The apprentice.

Adam Nathaniel Burns. Rachel found him.

Pause.

Rickman She found him?

Adam He is from a good Quaker family.

Rickman Let me oversee this for you. Will you send him to me? Let me speak with him.

Adam Thank you, James.

Pause.

And I will endeavour to keep Rachel close.

Rickman You are a good husband to her. Tell her to weigh her words, Friend. Let her find stillness before she takes utterance. It will help her.

Adam She is suffering. Not to be blessed with children –

Rickman Suffering can bring us closer to God – if we do not resist it.

Pause.

You are a valued member of our community, Adam. Our cornerstone. I will hold you both in my prayers.

He exits.

SCENE SEVEN

Exterior.
    Adam enters, wearing a work belt and tools. He manoeuvres a large stone into place. Nathaniel enters. Watches him.

Nathaniel This work has made you strong.

Adam says nothing, takes out tools from his belt. He prepares to work.

Adam You spoke with James?

Nathaniel I met with the elder and his family. He welcomes me with open arms.

Adam nods.

Adam Then it is time for you to learn . . . Firstly we must work the stone. They say that stones are cold. But here, feel.

Nathaniel touches the stone.

Warm from the sun. They say that stones are mute, but if you work with them long enough, they speak to you. They tell you the cracks, the breaks, teach you how to

fashion them. Once you understand them, they are soft
and malleable as honeycomb.

He hands him a work tool.

The stone will teach us how we must be with it.

*Adam 'works' the stone. Then he looks to Nathaniel.
After a moment, under Adam's watchful eye,
Nathaniel works the stone too.*

Nathaniel Is Rachel feeling better?

Adam She is resting.

Nathaniel I admired her at Meeting. She has a rare
eloquence.

*Adam says nothing, keeps working. Nathaniel sets to
work again.*

I thought our work was tombstones. The graves of the
dead?

Adam We will come to that. We create too – walls,
buildings, monuments –

Nathaniel But it is the wars that keep us busy?

Adam stops, looks at him.

Adam Do you judge me?

Nathaniel No, Adam.

Adam lays aside his tools for a moment, troubled.

Adam My Father was a Quaker. He was attacked for his
conscience. For not paying his taxes. For refusing to
fight . . . It is hard to live like this . . . I believe in the
testimony with all my heart but sometimes our peaceful-
ness does feel like – a repudiation rather than a force in
itself. It is a beginning, I know, but I wonder where it will
lead, if anywhere . . . I have no sons and sometimes I feel

the lack of them – like a punishment. I wonder if it is my punishment.

Nathaniel From God?

Adam God does not punish me. My mind does.

Nathaniel I find it hard to turn the other cheek. Sometimes I cannot trust myself . . . I think if I were recruited, I would desert rather than fight.

Adam looks at him.

Adam We must hold on to the truth. We must win over the enemy with the force of our love.

He starts to work. Stops.

The wars keep us busy, yes. Men are dying and they do not know what for. But I have a cause. I will build a proper Meeting House. One day. Soon. A place to worship. A meeting place for all to come. The tombs of the good dead will pay for it. That is how I square my conscience to it. Come, let us work.

Nathaniel nods. They work on.

Nathaniel It's hot work.

He takes off his shirt. He's bare-chested. He works on. Adam stops and looks at him. He stares at his back.

Adam You have a wound.

Nathaniel I fell. When I was a child.

Adam stares at him again – unsure about this explanation. Nathaniel holds his stare. Adam looks down.

Are not you hot?

Adam turns back to the stone.

Adam I am used to it.

They work. Suddenly Adam stops. Without looking at Nathaniel he takes off his shirt too. Nathaniel doesn't stop what he's doing. Adam starts to work again.

It is good. To have company. I was solitary before.

Nathaniel smiles. They work on.

SCENE EIGHT

Biddy and Tabitha enter and pass the men – Tabitha ogles them and Biddy pulls her along. Nathaniel and Adam gather up their tools and exit.

Biddy Don't be after asking me for hoops!

Tabitha But Mamma!

Biddy What would your father say to hoops in your petticoats? It would put him in an early grave.

Tabitha Why must it always be plain dress?

Biddy Because lace and ornament will not make you happy. You have no need of decoration.

Rachel greets them as Alice gets the blanket-box of linen.

Rachel Friend Biddy.

Biddy The trials of being a mother, Rachel!

Rachel (*quietly*) I would not know.

Biddy You look pale, Friend.

Rachel (*avoiding her eyes*) I do not sleep. Come, Tabitha, Mamma must make you this dress.

Alice takes out a large white sheet and places it against Tabitha's back. Tabitha is fidgety.

37

Alice *Stand still. Stand up straight.*

Rachel She needs you to stand up straight, Tabitha.

Alice starts to make her tailor's marks on the cloth. She's absorbed in her task.

Tabitha (*referring to Alice*) Has she always been like this?

Rachel What do you mean?

Biddy Tabby.

Tabitha Deaf and dumb.

Rachel She is not dumb.

Tabitha But she can't talk. And she is stone deaf.

Rachel Alice could hear when she was born. But she had scarlet fever when she was two. One morning she woke up deaf.

She interprets for her mother:

You woke up deaf.

Alice *The birds came when I was sleeping.*

Rachel smiles.

Tabitha What did she say?

Rachel She said the birds took her hearing away.

Tabitha The birds?

Rachel It's something her mother told her. A tale.

Tabitha Why would she say that?

Rachel Because she could not bear to think of God having a hand in it.

Rachel helps her mother with preparing the dress.

My grandparents were rich. They sent her away to a school for the deaf. She learned to speak with her hands. They tried to teach her to talk – indeed she can talk.

Tabitha Let her say something! Oh do!

Rachel (*shaking her head*) She is ashamed of the noises her throat makes. She has no mastery of them. But my dear father saw her for what she is. He knew the depths of her thinking.

Tabitha You are rich, Rachel! But why would you live here then?

Biddy Tabitha!

Rachel (*shakes her head*) We are not rich. My mother's brother inherited all. Save this box. My father was a schoolteacher, and after he died we were forced to fend for ourselves. I used to sell my mother's sewing in the marketplace. Till I met Adam there one day.

She smiles at the memory.

Biddy Well, your mother's been blessed with her hands at any rate! What a fine seamstress you are, Alice. Oh that's nice cloth, Tabby. It looks lovely next your skin. She has skin like silk, does she not?

Rachel *Mamma – here.*

She hands her mother the chalk. Rachel holds the sheet against Tabitha, while Alice makes marks to show her where she must cut.

Biddy Maybe we could tease the neckline a little –

Rachel *Lower, Mamma.*

Biddy And perhaps a pulling in at her waist. She has such a slender waist. It would be a shame not to show it off. And perhaps the hem can be a shade above her shoe.

Rachel *Higher, Mamma.*

Alice tuts and adjusts the length of the skirt so it rises high up Tabitha's leg. The women laugh.

Tabitha Oh yes, Mamma! I do hate plain dress with all my heart.

Biddy Let her toes peep out at the very least, Good Alice. The elder will barely notice! She does have such dear ankles. It is a shame to eschew all fashion. For the young ones at least. You and I are past all that frippery, Rachel. But she must ensnare a husband yet. We must allow her some weapons in her armoury.

Rachel You might choose a more quakerly metaphor, Biddy.

Biddy Oh well, I am not a woman of words like you, Rachel.

Rachel No, you are not . . . I suppose your husband is angry with me.

Biddy He prays for you. We all pray for you.

Rachel I do not want your prayers.

Biddy I wouldn't have the courage to stand there and speak like you do.

Rachel Maybe you should, Biddy. It seems to me there are some things you'd as well to unburden yourself of.

Biddy What do you mean?

Rachel A world where words are stifled is a world of fear.

Biddy And yet words can be weapons, Friend. Words can leave scars just as readily as knives can.

Rachel stares at Biddy, who turns away. Alice turns Tabitha round to do the back of the dress. Adam and

Nathaniel enter, still bare-chested. Tabitha giggles. Alice watches.

In the name of plainspeaking! Will you look at our Friends?

Rachel Adam. There is a child here.

Adam hastily puts his shirt back on. Nathaniel stays as he is.

Tabitha You must not mind me. We have a testimony to plain dress. Is Nathaniel Burns not as God Himself intended?

Nathaniel She speaks true. I am as plain as they come.

He winks at Tabitha. She giggles. Rachel watches.

Biddy Such impudence! Tabitha Rickman! Avert your eyes from this man's flesh. What am I to do with this girl? Apologise to our dear Friend from the North at once.

Rachel gets the water pitcher. Alice works and watches.

Tabitha I beg your pardon, Nathaniel Burns.

Biddy I said avert your eyes, girl!

Tabitha But you told me to address him!

Biddy Address him with your tongue, not undress him with your eyes!

Nathaniel You have nothing to be sorry for, Tabitha Rickman.

Rachel comes between Tabitha and Nathaniel and fills the pitcher with water.

Adam I'm sorry, Biddy. The sun is sharp today. The boy and I were hot and dusty from our work. Nathaniel. Remember your modesty.

Nathaniel I knew I had forgot something.

Adam throws Nathaniel his shirt, smiling at him. Nathaniel puts it on.

Biddy Tabitha, run along home before I tell Good Alice to tear your new frock to shreds. You are a disgrace to me and your poor Father. And you a birthright Quaker!

Tabitha Sorry, Mamma. Thank you, Good Alice. Rachel . . . Nathaniel Burns.

Biddy Tabitha!

Tabitha runs off. Adam watches her go.

Forgive her, Friends. She is of an age.

Adam She seems much older than she was.

Rachel Children grow, Adam.

Adam She is growing with great alacrity.

Biddy Her father can't keep up.

Adam She is comely.

Rachel Adam!

Adam What? I mean nothing by it! I have known dear Tabitha since she was a babe in arms.

Biddy He merely speaks the truth. She *is* comely. But it is kind of you to notice, Adam.

Nathaniel Adam looks at her merely with an artist's eye – as if he were to cast her in stone!

Adam Indeed, I do. My chisel in my hand.

Biddy shrieks with laughter.

Nathaniel A man can look, Rachel, without having any bad intentions –

Adam Indeed, are we not the most enlightened of all people for how we respect our womenfolk – are they not held equal, revered – do we not have a testimony to hold our dear daughters in the light?!

Nathaniel I hold them in the light as often as I can.

Adam laughs.

Adam Well spoken, young Friend.

Biddy Why, Adam Young, I've never known you so gay!

Rachel Having an apprentice has certainly loosened your tongue.

Nathaniel turns towards Rachel. Adam and Biddy are together.

Adam I am the most fortunate man, Friend Biddy. I need not look at other women for I am blessed with a beautiful wife.

Biddy I think Friend Rachel is the fortunate one.

Adam All other women fall down by compare!

Biddy Yes. She is lucky in you . . . But I am blessed in my James of course. And he can be most unquakerly in the midnight hour! He is a man of appetite when he so desires! I am sometimes pleased to hear the baby cry, so I am!

Adam I start to see the elder in a different light!

Nathaniel And who can blame him – you are all woman, Friend Biddy!

Biddy shrieks again.

Biddy Pray stop. This much mirth is not good for me. Oh! I shall rupture myself!

Rachel (*to Nathaniel*) Wash yourself. We will eat betimes.

Nathaniel As you wish it, Rachel.

He exits.

Biddy Oh, dear Adam. We do approve of your young apprentice! He has come several times to visit. Such good manners! So well-spoken!

Adam He learns fast.

Biddy And you are the man to teach him. What great fortune that the Lord delivered him straight to your doorstep! Proof if it were needed that our prayers are always attended to.

Adam Amen.

Biddy It is good to see this house full of laughter.

She is leaving.

We are so lucky in our community. With the world at large at war, and not a cross word between a single one of us! I think I shall be forced to sing my way home. Ha! Dear Friend, I hold you in the light.

The two women embrace.

Rachel As I do you.

Biddy (*to Alice*) Good Alice. Bless her.

Alice looks stonily at Biddy, as she leaves. During the next, she finishes up her preparations for the dress. Rachel watches Adam. He busies himself with tidying away his tools and work belt. He whistles happily.

Adam What have you prepared for your hungry menfolk, then, Alice? I could eat an ox.

She smiles uncomprehendingly at him.

Rachel You and the boy – you work well together?

Adam He applies himself.

Rachel He makes you happy.

Adam Would you not see me happy?

Rachel Of course. I only wish I were the source.

He stops, angry.

Adam Why do you do this?

Rachel What?

Adam You lay me traps. What is it you want me to say, Rachel? You brought him to me. You wanted him my apprentice. I thank you. He is what I hoped for.

Rachel Speak more quietly – He will hear –

Adam This is my house.

Rachel I will leave you to him then –

Adam Where are you going?

Rachel I need the air.

He grabs hold of her, she's shocked. Alice stands up.

Adam!

Adam You will not walk out of this house! You will not walk today!

Rachel You are hurting me.

Adam You will talk to me.

Rachel Let go of me.

Adam What? You have no words for me? You have words only when they are least wanted, least called for. I tell you not to speak, you speak. I urge you to talk and you are silent?

He sees Alice watching him. He lets go of Rachel. Walks away.

Rachel The 'elder' rebuked me again, did he not?

Adam You said you would try not to speak.

Rachel The words make me feel alive, Adam. Without them, I am dead.

Adam Do not paint yourself so. It is not truthful. You can find your faith in silence.

Rachel I find nothing in the silence except fear and pain. The words free me. They make me think I can be something. I am not a mother, Adam, that was denied me – I must be something – I must find a way of being – I must be useful –

Adam You can speak at home. To me. To Alice. But you cannot minister in the Meeting House.

Rachel What – so where can I minister? In the wilderness? Is that where you would send me?

Alice puts the cloth back in the blanket-box. She slams the lid for effect. To get their attention.

Adam Tell your mother to go.

Rachel She cannot hear us.

Adam She is watching me.

Rachel What is wrong in that?

Adam Why do you turn me in circles?

Rachel Why should she leave? Tell me why?

Adam What is this now, woman?

Rachel We have lived here for years and you will not learn to speak with her. You will not even try. None of

46

you. She has no voice in this community. She is denied ministry. How lonely do you think she is? It is no sin to be deaf, Adam.

Adam You need not tell me.

Rachel Stand up in Meeting then and tell them. For they all think her mute and enfeebled. The idiot in their midst. They smile at her and call her good but they think she has nothing to say. They do not know her power. You must stand up and acknowledge her.

Adam I will if you wish it.

Rachel Do it not for me. Do it for yourself. I do not want to tell you this. I want you to think it.

Alice (*signs*) *What is he saying? Is he talking about me? Tell me. Look at me.*

   Rachel ignores her.

Adam Talk to her. She is upset.

Rachel You talk to her. All my life I have had to speak for her. From the moment sound came from my mouth. Before I could walk! Before I could think for myself!

   Adam looks helplessly at Alice.

(*To Alice.*) *I'm tired.*

   She turns away. Alice signs back:

Alice *Show me your hands.*

Rachel Without me her thoughts are nothing – they go nowhere. She is denied the comfort of friendship.

Adam God hears her. God hears everything.

Rachel Then let Him relieve me of this burden. ***God make Mamma to hear.*** God give me my children. God make them live. God make me whole.

47

Adam You cannot ask these things –

Rachel Then what do I ask of God?! Tell me!

Adam We cannot question His ways.

Alice tries to get Rachel's attention.

Alice *Talk to me. Respect me. I am your Mamma.*

Rachel If I cannot ask this of God, tell me what to say, Adam. How do I speak to God? How do I speak to Him so He will listen? Do I speak to Him with my tongue or my hands? Do I speak to Him in Meeting? Or do I keep silent? I am lost, Adam. Teach me how I find God.

Adam Let your life speak, Rachel. Only this. Let your life speak.

Alice tries to attract her daughter's attention again. She stamps on the floor this time.

Rachel *Mamma, go. He does not want you here.*

Adam (*shaking his head, trying to communicate with her*) Alice – please, I would speak with Rachel . . . You should not have said that to her. You misrepresent me.

Rachel Now you know how it is all the time for her.

Alice looks at them both fiercely. Exits.

Adam Alice – wait.

Rachel I will attend to her.

Rachel follows her.

Adam I am sorry – wife. You are tired. We are both of us tired.

She stops. Relents a little.

Rachel I would let my life speak, I would. I try.

Adam I know you do.

Rachel I wish I could know my truth – I wish I could live in the centre of it as you do –

Adam Shhh. Now is not the time to fret. Let us eat. Call the boy and let us eat together.

Rachel I am not hungry.

Adam Rachel – you will not go to the town – I forbid it. I am your husband and I forbid it. Rachel! Please.

She picks up the white chalk, puts it in her pocket. She leaves. Adam buries his head in his hands.

SCENE NINE

The place of stones. Rachel is walking. She kneels before her children's graves. She takes a piece of chalk and writes her name beneath theirs. Nathaniel enters.

Nathaniel I dreamed about you last night.

Rachel You followed me here. Where is Adam?

Nathaniel Asleep in his chair. Snoring like a baby . . . I like this place . . . Who taught you to write? It is not common for a woman –

Rachel My father. He gave me all the means of language he could. As did my mother. I am burdened with too much language.

She rubs her name out.

Nathaniel Don't –

Rachel Adam might see it. He would be hurt.

Nathaniel Adam cannot read.

Rachel Don't talk of him like that.

Nathaniel I speak only the truth. So, do I make a good Quaker? I think I am a true seeker of the light!

Rachel Adam likes you.

Nathaniel He is a good man.

Rachel He is not as strong as he looks.

Pause.

Tabitha is very taken with you.

Nathaniel She is a child. You are a woman.

Rachel I am going –

Nathaniel When you spoke – at Meeting – I have never seen a woman speak like that.

Pause.

Rachel Your dream. Was it a nightmare? Are you still plagued with nightmares?

Nathaniel No, I sleep much better since I am with you.

She turns away from him.

You have your back to me. In my dream. I am looking at your neck. I can see there is a melancholy in you. And I am willing you to turn. To see me. But then I realise that you know that I am there. You are choosing not to turn.

Rachel Stop it! I don't trust your words.

Nathaniel Then let's speak without words. That way nothing can be said to have passed between us –

Rachel Nothing will pass between us –

Nathaniel Teach me the language of your hands. Like you speak with your mother.

Rachel I will not.

Nathaniel But why?

Pause.

Rachel The language of my hands is pure. Because it comes from my body as well as my mind. It is so much bigger than merely speaking. With my hands I cannot hide.

Nathaniel You want to hide your feelings from me. Why is that?!

Rachel I did not say that. You put words in my mouth.

Nathaniel Forgive me –

Rachel My signs are precious. They belong to me.

Nathaniel Then I will make my own signs up. You must try to understand them.

Rachel I am too old for your games.

He signs crudely.

Nathaniel *I – like you. I sleep – dream of you. Your speaking – touches me. I hear you.*

She smiles in spite of herself.

Rachel That means nothing. Your hands speak nonsense.

He thinks.

Nathaniel This is my sign for you. *Ra – chel.* A sign for a rainbow – and a bird rising up. A little chel bird. *Ra – chel.* That's good, isn't it? Do you have a sign for me?

Rachel No.

Nathaniel You do. I saw it.

He makes the sign of loss.

Rachel (*sharp*) That sign is not for you.

Nathaniel I know you have suffered. I want to help you. Think of a new sign. A sign for me. Nathaniel. The new Nathaniel. Please.

She thinks. She signs. Perhaps we see her hands pitter-pattering like rain out of her mouth up and over a hill.

I like it. Thank you. You have given me a precious thing.

Rachel *Nathaniel.* Who are you?

Nathaniel You know who I am. You were waiting for me.

Pause.

Rachel.

Pause.

Rachel *Nathaniel.*

They sign at the same time.

Nathaniel *Rachel.*

Rachel *Nathaniel.*

They stare at each other. Then he bends and takes a piece of chalk from the ground. He draws on her body. A line from her throat. Through her chest. To her belly. She takes a piece of chalk and draws on his body. Across his chest. And then down. A large cross. They draw ever closer. They draw on each other's backs. Lines. Circles. They possess each other. At last they kiss. They begin to make love. Lights fade.

End of Act One.

Act Two

SCENE ONE

*The whole community apart from Rachel sit in Meeting.
Silence. Then Rickman turns to the person next to him
and shakes their hand. Everyone follows suit. Rickman
nods goodbye to Biddy and Tabitha and looks for Adam.
Adam gets up to go.*

Rickman Adam – a whole Meeting in silence! It restores
the soul.

Adam I must get back – Rachel will be waiting for me.

Rickman Can I walk with you, Friend?

Adam and Rickman fall into step.

Adam What news of the war?

Rickman It is coming ever closer. They are building
fortifications at the coast. Not seven miles from here. All
the talk is of invasion. The country is on high alert.

Adam The numbers of dead and injured must be terrible.
On both sides.

Rickman Yearly Meeting is making plans to provide
relief for the innocent victims. But in the meantime
everyone walks on tinder. There have been skirmishes
with our people elsewhere in the country, persecution,
injuries sustained. The mood is angry. We are seen as
traitors. Now more than ever we must keep our
community safe – no one should walk out alone now,
particularly at night.

Adam No.

Rickman Adam. I have been thinking about Friend Rachel –

Adam I spoke with her as you instructed me –

Rickman She has not been at Meeting this past month.

Adam She is at home. She is sick.

Rickman It grieves me to hear it.

Adam She will come when she is able –

Rickman Forgive me. I do not mean to berate her. We miss her presence among us.

Adam I will tell her so.

Rickman I have been thinking – I fear I was too harsh on her. Her ministry does not speak to me but that does not mean that it does not touch the hearts of other Friends.

Adam No indeed.

Rickman I have an important task I would like to entrust to her. There are some duties that fall more naturally to a woman's hands. I would have Rachel more actively engaged in the pastoral care of our community – I think this will lighten her burden. She must not feel that she is excluded in any way from us, because she was not born to us. She is an integral part of us and we hold her in the light.

Adam Thank you, James. She has a calling for service – I think this will help her. I will speak with her.

Rickman Blessing upon blessing.

He departs. A moment, then Adam exits.

The house. Alice is there with a washing bowl and cloth. She pounds the cloth angrily. Rachel enters with cutlery for the table. She looks at her mother.

Rachel *You are very quiet.*

Alice turns her back on Rachel, continues with her work.

Have I hurt you? What is my misdemeanour?

Pause. Rachel looks at her mother.

You punish me, do you? But I am already punished, Mother. Your silence has punished me since the day I was born.

She lays the table. She doesn't hear Nathaniel enter.

When I was a girl I prayed for a man who would listen to me all day and all night. So I could talk and talk and talk. He would swallow up all my thoughts . . . He would be unafraid of me – of who I am. The girl who speaks with her voice and with her hands. He would have an answer for everything.

Pause.

I hoped there would be no silence between us. Never any silence.

Nathaniel I hear you, Friend.

Rachel spins round. Alice hasn't noticed him.

Rachel Get out! We must not be alone together.

Nathaniel Don't fret. Your mother is here. We are safe.

During the next Alice notices them.

Rachel Adam is not here.

Nathaniel He is foolish to leave you alone.

Rachel I do not want this.

Nathaniel You lie.

He touches Rachel's face. Alice takes the pitcher of water and throws it at him. He's soaked.

Rachel Mother! *What are you doing?*

Alice *Me? It's you. Be careful!*

She exits. Nathaniel laughs.

Nathaniel Good Alice! Well, well, well. She has sniffed us out. She is sharp as a pin! Lucky for us she cannot speak!

He takes off his sodden shirt, dries himself. She turns away from him.

Rachel You must go.

Nathaniel What, are you shy of my body now? It is late for that.

Rachel What passed between us was wrong. It will not happen again.

Nathaniel I think of it all the time – your skin next to mine –

She goes and fetches him a clean shirt.

Rachel You must leave this place.

He puts his shirt on calmly.

My mother will not speak to me. You have come between me and my husband. I cannot go to Meeting. I am without God. You have made me hate myself. I beg you – leave this place. Say your father has ordered your return.

Nathaniel I will go if you wish it.

Rachel I will make your excuses –

Nathaniel But I do not wish to go . . . Tell me there was not truth in what we did?

Rachel You must return to your barracks.

Nathaniel I cannot return . . . I am a coward. And a deserter. I deserted my regiment.

Rachel You did not tell me this.

Nathaniel If I go back I will be arrested. Tried. Killed. At the very least they will transport me.

Pause.

Rachel Tell them you would lay down your arms. Tell them you are a Quaker. Tell them your conscience objects.

Nathaniel (*laughs*) They would rather kill me than listen to my conscience. You have no idea –

Rachel But you are only a boy –

Nathaniel (*a hint of desperation*) I cannot fight, Rachel. I cannot kill any more men. Please. You send me off, you send me to die.

Rachel Don't say that –

Nathaniel I will not touch you again. I promise.

Rachel But we have what has happened in our hearts – we carry it with us –

Nathaniel I know how to fight – this is all I have learned. Teach me how to be different. I respect you, Rachel. I will never speak of what happened between us. I swear! I respect Adam too. He is like a father to me. I have never known love, not like the love of you and Adam. Please. I beg you. Let this be my home.

Rachel Nathaniel –

Nathaniel I want nothing more from you but you hold me in the light.

Pause.

Rachel Forgive me – I thought only of myself – I do know how much you have suffered –

She touches his face. He takes her hand, kisses it. Adam enters. Rachel withdraws her hand.

Adam!

Nathaniel Your wife comforts me, Friend.

Adam looks at Rachel.

Rachel He misses his late mother.

Adam Of course.

Rachel goes to Adam and puts her arms around him. Nathaniel looks away.

(*Surprised, a little embarrassed.*) Rachel!

She goes to exit. He holds her back.

Where are you going?

Rachel (*tense*) I am going to prepare the meal.

He nods. She exits.

Adam My wife feels things deeply.

Nathaniel She is a woman of compassion.

Adam She gave birth to three sons. But they died all three.

Nathaniel I did not know this. I am heartsick for her.

Adam She walks. She visits their graves. When she is troubled. I wish she would not. I would keep her at home.

Nathaniel Will you not walk with her?

Adam Sometimes it is hard between us. I am a reminder of the sorrow.

Pause.

I mourn them too.

Pause.

It is good you have a bond. You and my wife.

Pause.

Friend. I cannot be with Rachel every moment – I would ask you to watch her when I cannot. Follow her if she walks. Keep her company. There are people who are against us, who would think nothing of killing one of our number.

Nathaniel I will do this for you.

He goes to exit.

Adam And if you are sad, you can come to me.

Nathaniel I will, Friend.

Adam I hope I do not speak out of turn. I say this only because your father is not here.

Nathaniel (*sincere*) You are a better father to me, Adam, than he ever was.

Adam looks at him. Touched.

(*Saying this for the first time.*) I – I hold you in the light, Adam.

Nathaniel smiles at him and exits. Adam is left, overcome.

*Alice brings food and places it on the table before Adam.
Rachel enters with water. She glances at her mother. The
air is still strained between the two women.*

Rachel Is Biddy coming with the elder?

Adam James said it was a private matter –

Rachel If it is a private matter then Biddy will come.

Adam Nothing will stop her. It is true.

They smile.

I love to see you smile.

Rachel I smile for you, husband.

Adam Where is the boy?

Rachel stops smiling.

Rachel He has gone out. I am not his keeper, Adam.

Adam He is young – he needs his freedom . . . I think
he is shy of the elders. I was too at his age. Have you
noticed he never speaks in Meeting? He seems deep in
prayer.

*Rachel says nothing, busies herself with preparing the
table.*

He progresses well in his work. I will set him to carving
the names soon – the inscription.

Rachel He makes himself indispensable to you.

Adam We laugh too. It is good with the nature of our
work.

Pause.

He is like me – when I was an apprentice.

Alice walks past Rachel. Rachel is making an effort with her.

Rachel *Mamma? Are you well? Your hands? Do they ail?*

Alice shakes her head, not wanting to converse. She takes out Tabitha's dress – it's almost finished – holds it up.

Beautiful . . . You will eat with us?

Alice shakes her head. Sits and starts to sew. Voices off. Biddy enters with her baby, followed by Rickman. Rickman and Adam shake hands.

Biddy Friend Adam! What a beautiful day! Not a cloud in the sky. Oh, and we are to eat too! And you not well, Rachel. We did not mean to put you to trouble –

Rachel It is no trouble.

Biddy Now where can I put this blessed child down so I can eat?

Rachel Mamma will look after her. *Mamma you can keep the baby, while we eat?*

Alice smiles and puts her hands out.

Biddy Can she be trusted?

Rickman Bedelia. Give Alice the baby.

Biddy Yes, of course, Good Alice. Mind her head – tell her to mind her head. Tell her, Rachel!

Rachel does not tell her. Alice takes the baby, smiles and nods at Biddy.

It's only she is a little fractious. She is to cut a tooth. Good Alice may not hear her.

Rachel She certainly will not hear her.

Rickman But we will hear her.

Biddy Don't look at me like that. Friend Rachel told me – she had to learn not to cry – is it not so, Rachel? – It pained me to hear it – when you were a baby?

Pause.

Rachel My mother attended to all my needs. But it is true I learned not to cry. I would tug on her shoulder instead.

Adam She is still not in the habit of crying.

Rachel Adam.

Biddy Oh, I love to cry! I revel in it altogether sometimes!

Rachel I was fortunate. My mother had strong shoulders.

Alice makes a strange clicking noise. She delights in the baby. They all look at her. Biddy is rather repulsed.

Rickman What a thing.

Adam Shall we sit?

They sit.

Rickman We are here on Quaker business.

Biddy Indeed. I am bursting to tell you!

Rickman Contain yourself, Bedelia. Shall we say grace?

They bow their heads for a moment in silence. Alice rocks the baby. She makes plosive voiceless sounds to the baby. Rickman looks up, frowns – goes to censure her but then checks himself. She looks at him. He smiles at her.

Amen.

Adam breaks bread for them.

Friend Rachel, I am here to ask a favour of you. There is a young woman in the Meeting – I would ask you to make an enquiry regarding her clearness.

Biddy Although she is clear as the sky!

Rachel Someone is to marry?

Rickman Indeed, in these troubled times it brings a glimmer of hope. I would nominate you as the Friend who will report on whether she is clear of all others and free to pursue her intentions.

Biddy Will you do it, Rachel?

Rachel (*confused*) Of course.

Biddy Let me tell her who it is! No, you must guess! It is Tabitha! My little Tabitha! A wife!

Adam Tabitha! Well then, there can be no doubts as to her clearness!

Biddy I know!

Adam I wish we had some wine. This is a cause for celebration.

Rickman Thank you, Adam. Within the bounds of modest propriety, I believe it is!

Adam And who is the lucky man?

Rickman It is your apprentice, Adam. Who else?!

Alice senses something is wrong. Rachel drinks her water. Adam laughs.

Adam I thought there was a spring in his step of late!

Biddy He has conducted their courtship, brief as it is, like a dream. I have been present throughout – I was so desirous of telling you, Rachel, but the elder here told me to bite my tongue till we knew the outcome of his attentions. Nathaniel is a young man of such propriety and good intentions and piety too of course. Eminent piety. He is a credit to his family. And to you too.

Rachel They have known each other such a short time.

Rickman The boy is from a good Quaker family. I hope, Adam, that it does not interfere with the terms of his apprenticeship.

Adam No indeed. Married men have more reason to work. As long as he is up betimes –

Biddy Perhaps the first day of their married life we can allow him the morning off!

Rickman (*gently chiding*) Biddy!

Rachel Is the date set?

Rickman Once you have satisfied us that they are clear in their intentions to marry, I see no reason to delay it! We can post an announcement and proceed as our dear founders instructed us. We marry none here – we are but witnesses to the Lord's work!

Biddy You must make a start, Rachel. My Tabby is desperate to wed.

Rachel (*worried*) Where will they live? After they are married? Alice must keep her room –

Adam We can accommodate them.

Rachel But if they have children –

Pause.

Adam Would it not be a blessing?

Rachel What of the groom's clearness? How can we be satisfied that the groom is free to marry?

Rickman Nathaniel has furnished me with a letter from his father. Alas, poor man, he ails and may not travel to the wedding. But he sends his blessing and letters of commendation. Impeccable references for the boy.

Rachel It is not usual to be satisfied by a letter.

Rickman It is down to the discretion of the elders. I am satisfied. We are few in number here. It is within our interests to welcome new Friends. It strengthens us.

Adam He spoke of a brother.

Rickman Abroad for reasons of trade.

Rachel So he will be unrepresented at the wedding? None of his family will be present?

Adam We are his family now. We will represent him.

Pause.

Biddy You act strangely, Rachel. I had hoped you would share in my joy.

Rachel stands up and falters.

Rachel Excuse me – I don't feel well!

Adam (*solicitous*) Wife?

Rickman Perhaps this enquiry will tax her too much.

Rachel No, no. I do it willingly. Excuse me.

Rickman I hope we will see you at Meeting this Sunday, Rachel.

She nods and exits. Alice gives Biddy the baby.

Biddy Thank you, Good Alice. Will you look at that? Sleeping soundly.

Alice starts to clear the table.

Rickman I hope Rachel is cheered by our news.

Biddy She should be happy for me. For my Tabitha.

Adam She is surprised. The boy is – like a son to her.

Rickman Of course.

Biddy (*critical*) But he is not her son.

Rickman Biddy worries so much for Rachel. Perhaps you should bear witness to Rachel's enquiries into Tabitha's clearness. Lend her your support, wife.

Biddy Indeed I will.

Rickman The workings of the human heart are mysterious. Farewell, Friend.

Adam I will see you out.

Rickman and Adam shake hands formally and exit.

SCENE FOUR

Music. All take their place for Meeting. Rachel runs in late to the Meeting. She looks unkempt – as if she is sleepwalking. She sits and then stands again immediately. The others remain with their heads bowed.

Rachel Friends. I have been searching for a stone – a small white stone. To fit in my palm. Does not the Bible tell us: 'To him that overcometh will I give a white stone. And in the stone a new name written.' I am so desirous of a new name. The stone will speak my name when I can no longer speak, you see. When I am dead and gone. Oh! But I am afraid to die. I am so afraid! For I have no children. I have done nothing. Is it a sin to want to be heard? But if I have the stone then they will know my name. I want them all to read my name. Adam! You will make them do this – after I am dead. So that they will know that I lived. That I spoke up – even if no one would heed me. I feel such shame! Why is that? But my dying will redeem me. My name in stone. Adam. If God will not do this for me then you will? Please, Adam.

66

She sits next to Adam. He turns and shakes hands with her, smiling. Everyone else shakes hands.

Adam What is it, Rachel?

Rachel Adam. I tried not to speak in Meeting. I really tried. But the words would still come – I could not stop them. I do not know what I was saying –

Adam Wife! You did not speak.

Rachel What?

Adam You were as silent as flint.

Rachel No. I spoke –

Adam You did not. I give you my word.

Rachel But I know I spoke!

Adam These are your imaginings, wife. Nothing more.

Adam kisses her. Rachel stands there, confused. Her hair and face wild. The men all leave.

SCENE FIVE

Tabitha stands before Rachel. Rachel tries to focus on her. She is struggling with her emotions, her thoughts.

Rachel Friend Tabitha? What –? Ah yes. I must make enquiries into your clearness.

Biddy approaches. She has her baby with her. She lays her down in a nest of blankets during the next.

Biddy We know you are free from all others. The enquiry is but a formality, Tabby.

The dress fitting: during the next Alice takes out the dress she has been making from the blanket-box and dresses Tabitha.

Tabitha Does the dress become me?

Biddy Nathaniel will be falling over himself to say his vows.

Rachel This is your wedding dress? But the marriage is not decided yet.

Biddy Of course the marriage is decided. The Lord has decided.

Rachel No – no, wait! Let me discharge my duty, Biddy. Let me speak with her alone.

Biddy James would have me witness you.

Rachel But why?

Biddy I cannot question the elder's thinking.

    Pause.

Rachel You are very young, Tabby.

Biddy She is young but she knows her mind . . . You were late to wed as I recall, Rachel.

Rachel (*to Tabitha*) Are you sure this is what you want?

Tabitha (*playing with her dress*) Of course, Rachel. Mamma, do you think Pappa will allow me curls in my hair on my wedding day?

Biddy He will have me to answer to if he does not.

Rachel Tabitha. What do you feel – when you are with Nathaniel? In your body?

Tabitha I feel my heart fluttering in my chest. Like a bird trapped in a tower.

Biddy Bless her. I can remember that feeling.

Rachel Tabby, are you convinced of Nathaniel's good intentions?

Tabitha What mean you?

Rachel We've known him such a short time! Nathaniel is a stranger to us.

Biddy He is a Friend.

Rachel We know nothing of his background.

Biddy Her father is satisfied.

Rachel (*turning to Tabitha*) Perhaps we should exercise some caution. There is no rush, Tabitha – you are so young! I think your father should visit with his father.

Biddy The elder does not doubt Nathaniel. Friend Rachel, may I be frank? He doubts you more than the boy.

   Pause.

Rachel Why do you say this, Biddy? It pains me.

Biddy You take no joy in my Tabitha's good luck. Anyone would think you do not want this marriage to happen. I know the boy is like a son to you. I do not want to see my Tabitha go – but a mother must learn to give up her children –

Rachel (*roughly*) You do not need to teach me this lesson.

Biddy Tabitha. Attend to your sister.

   Tabitha goes and plays with the baby. Alice watches the following.

You have your man, Rachel. Have the good grace to allow Tabitha hers.

Rachel I wish only to protect your daughter, Biddy.

Biddy I can protect my children. I do not need your assistance, Friend.

Rachel turns away.

I do not know you these days.

Rachel What do you mean?

Biddy With your wild talking and walking – you make it hard for me to love you.

Pause.

Rachel You have never forgiven me, have you, Biddy?

Biddy What?

Rachel That Adam chose me. He would not have you.

Biddy stares at Rachel, hurt, tearful.

Biddy Adam told you?

Rachel We are husband and wife.

Biddy Tabitha, come. We are leaving.

Rachel Forgive me, Biddy. I spoke out of turn.

Biddy spins round.

Biddy He should have chosen me. I would have borne him children.

Pause. Rachel feels the full brunt of this.

Rachel (*quietly*) She is clear. I will inform the Meeting.

Biddy and Tabitha exit.

SCENE SIX

Music. The place of stones. Alice exits. Rachel tends to her sons' graves – cold and alone. The wind is whooshing through the place.
Nathaniel enters. He stares at Rachel from behind.

Nathaniel I know you know I am here. You are choosing not to turn. I know you well.

She turns round angrily.

Rachel What do you want from me?

Nathaniel You must tell me how to be. When I marry Tabitha. The marriage ceremony. What I must say. You must teach me your customs. I would not fall out of step.

Rachel laughs incredulously.

Rachel Why would I do this for you?

Nathaniel You do not want me. I must find my bed elsewhere.

Rachel You are heartless.

Nathaniel I owe you nothing. It was but one night between us. Tabitha is young. We will have a life together. Children.

Pause.

Rachel And I must live forever in silence with the weight of what has passed between us.

Nathaniel I am trying to live in the light. As you are. This is my chance. I have the right to seize it.

Rachel You have no rights. This marriage is built on untruths. You are no Quaker –

Nathaniel And neither are you.

Rachel You cannot live in peace and unity with us. You do not belong.

Nathaniel Adam welcomed me into your home.

Rachel I will discover you. I will stand up in Meeting and disclose the truth. Who you are. What you have done to me.

Nathaniel (*laughs*) What I have done to you? What? There was no need on your side? No desire? Did you not seduce me with your hands? Talk to me with your hands so no one but I could understand? A young impressionable boy, a motherless boy. Did you not then betray your husband, the rock, who has stood beside you? You were innocent in all? Oh yes.

Rachel Why do you send me mad like this? You delight in it –

Nathaniel I am holding a mirror up to you, Rachel. That is all.

Rachel I will tell them that you are a liar, a soldier, a deserter.

Nathaniel Your life is already ruined. Would you ruin the life of young Tabitha too? Pretty, innocent Tabitha whom you have known since she was a child. The elder's daughter, no less. Does not the bitterness you harbour at the death of your own children turn you against another blameless child?

Rachel You are wicked.

Nathaniel I am thinking of you. I can see no happy end to this. You will be turned out of the community. You and your deaf mother. Then where will you go? You will not find another Adam.

Rachel I do not care. I will tell the truth. I will stand up in Meeting and I will speak –

Nathaniel You will not speak! You do not have the courage to sacrifice yourself. And even if you did speak – as I recall your word is not exactly taken as Gospel. I would safeguard your interests, Mrs Young, if I were you.

He makes to go.

Rachel Do you hate me? Is that it?

He stops.

I have no claims over you. I know this. But I thought you held me in the light. Now it seems you want to hurt me. Yet – when you met me you made a choice – to live with me, to lie with me. You made a choice.

Nathaniel There is no choosing, Rachel. There is only chance. We met. There was our meeting. Only that.

He goes to leave. He stops when she speaks.

Rachel You would know the right words to say? On your wedding day?

Pause.

You sit in silence. Till one of you is moved to speak . . . If you love her, if you feel the spirit within you, then you must stand up. And you must speak your promises. Your declarations of love. Before your community. Before God . . . But you can also decide not to speak.

Nathaniel I am indebted to you.

He leaves. She stands there. In another part of the stage Adam enters, takes off his belt and lies down to sleep.

SCENE SEVEN

Alice enters and sees Adam sleeping. She takes a blanket and gently places it over him. She leaves him to sleep, exits. After a moment, Rachel enters in a nightgown, carrying a candle. She goes to Adam.

Rachel Are you asleep?

Silence. She sits beside him.

When I was a baby I was alone in the darkness. Before
I learned to speak with my hands. It was not her fault.
But I remember it. I feel it in my body. The aloneness.
A red ribbon between me and nothingness. But then I met
you and I thought that the nothingness had gone forever.
But it is only a ribbon's width away. It is the nothingness
I fear most.

Adam God is in the nothingness.

Pause. She touches him. He kisses her hand.

You are late.

Rachel Is the boy here?

Adam Asleep in his bed.

Pause.

Rachel I cannot go to the wedding.

Adam Rachel –

Rachel I must tell you something now. It is the hardest
thing I will ever say. I have sinned. Against God and
against you.

Adam Let him who is without sin –

Rachel Listen to me. I lay with the boy. One time only.
I was seduced – by his words. I wanted to be – outside
my –

She puts her head in her hands. Silence.

Will you speak to me?

Pause.

Adam Do you love him?

Rachel I love you.

Adam Do you love him?

Rachel I love him and hate him as I love and hate myself.

Adam (*angry*) Did he hurt you?

Rachel No.

Adam Why did you do this? He is a boy!

Pause.

He is my apprentice!

Pause.

Have I not been everything to you? If you did not want me, you should have gone. Left me. If you want the town, then go to the town. Do not tear my heart in two like this. Why do you do this to me?

Silence.

Rachel You must speak out against me.

Adam What?

Rachel Tomorrow they marry. You must denounce me. Before God. Before the elders. Before our Friends. Let them all know who I am.

Adam And prevent the marriage?

Rachel Yes! But you must say it was my doing. That he was an innocent in all. You must let my life speak for me. This is what I want.

Adam You will be disowned.

Rachel But you will not.

Adam Would you leave me then?

Rachel It is what I deserve.

Adam What of your mother?

Rachel All I have left is my truth. He would rob me of that. But it is all I have left.

Adam And what of my truth? What of my love for you?

She puts her head in her hands.

He has betrayed me. The boy. I met him with love – and he has betrayed me. I would kill him –

Rachel Adam –

Adam Be quiet, woman. You have said what you have to say. Now I must think.

He gets up and walks towards the door.

Rachel Where are you going?

Adam To walk.

He exits. Rachel is in despair. She sinks down on the ground. Alice enters, concerned. She has just seen Adam exit. She goes and kneels by her daughter. Rachel does not look at Alice, but she knows that she is there. After a moment she reaches out and tugs on her shoulder. She tugs and tugs on her shoulder.

Rachel I want to die.

She is doubled up in pain.

Alice *What is wrong?*

Rachel doesn't reply.

The boy.

Rachel shakes her head.

Rachel It's not the boy. It's me.

Alice *The boy is nothing. He is not worthy of you. He is weak. He breaks everything. My Rachel is strong. My Rachel can rise above.*

Rachel No. I am not strong.

Alice draws her to her, rocks her.

SCENE EIGHT

*The wedding. The Friends are gathered. Biddy enters
with Rickman. They take their seats. Alice enters,
followed by Adam and Rachel. Adam is holding on to
Rachel's arm. She looks down at the floor. Finally
Nathaniel and Tabitha enter – Tabitha is in her new
dress. They take their seats. Alice glares at Nathaniel.
Rachel leans into Adam with her eyes closed. Silence.
Rickman stands.*

Rickman Friends, we are gathered before God to witness
the union of Friend Nathaniel Burns and Friend Tabitha
Rickman.

*He smiles at his daughter and sits. Pause. Tabitha
stands up, excited to say her vows.*

Tabitha Friends, in the presence of God I take this my
Friend Nathaniel Burns to be my husband!

She sits down, then remembers herself, stands again.

Promising through God's help to be unto him a faithful
wife, so long as we both on earth shall live!

*She sits, flustered. The congregation smile. Nathaniel
looks at her. Silence. Then Nathaniel looks at Rachel.
Rachel is still looking at her feet. Adam looks steadily
at Nathaniel. Nathaniel looks away. Biddy and Tabitha
exchange looks, worried that Nathaniel hasn't said his
vows.*

Out of the silence, Adam stands.

Adam Stand with me, Rachel.

This is untoward. Rachel is surprised, unsure. He pulls her up to stand beside him.

We welcomed Nathaniel Burns into our home but three months ago . . . such a short time –

Rachel looks searchingly at Adam.

(*With difficulty.*) My wife Rachel – would have me speak for her – my wife – my Rachel . . . Who has taught me what it is to love. Rachel and I would be the first Friends to wish Nathaniel and Tabitha peace and unity in their married life.

Rachel looks at Adam. She is shaking her head almost involuntarily. He smiles at her. He helps her to sit. Nathaniel stands.

Nathaniel Friends! I take this my Friend Tabitha Rickman to be my wife!

Music and an explosion of life. Nathaniel and Tabitha are exalted in some way by the Meeting. The moment is held. Rachel and Adam have not moved. Rachel turns to Adam.

Rachel Husband?

Adam I would not lose you for all the world.

Rachel You are too good.

Adam We will leave this place tonight.

Rachel But these are your people.

Adam We will find another community. The three of us. Alice, go home and pack our things.

Rachel *Go home, Mamma. Pack our things. We leave tonight.*

Alice nods and exits. Rachel watches as Nathaniel kisses Tabitha – a long, sultry kiss. Adam is shaking

78

*Rickman's hands. Biddy is happy. Adam goes to
congratulate her. She holds on to him for a moment
too long as Rickman goes to embrace his daughter.
Adam is surprised.*

Biddy This could have been us, Adam.

Adam (*gently*) Oh Biddy, you live in in the past, Friend.

*He walks away from her. At the same time Rachel tries
to leave. Nathaniel blocks her way. Biddy watches.*

Nathaniel *Ra–chel. Ra–chel.* I am talking to you, Rachel.
Will you not congratulate me?

Rachel I have to go – but I wish you peace, Friend.

Nathaniel *Rachel. Nathaniel.* Isn't that how it went?

Rachel Please do not mock me. Nathaniel –

Nathaniel Nathaniel is not my real name. I stole it. I saw
the name on a gravestone as I walked to this place. A
child's gravestone.

*Rachel stares at him aghast. She slaps him hard across
the face. Biddy approaches.*

Biddy Is this any way to congratulate the groom?

Nathaniel (*nursing his face*) She likes to speak with her
hands. Did you know that, Biddy, Mrs Young taught me
to speak with my hands. Is not that so?

Rachel says nothing. Biddy stares at her oddly.

Biddy Why did you do that?

Nathaniel I was her apprentice, isn't that right, Rachel?
So. Is my apprenticeship over? Or might we take one
more lesson –

Rachel Excuse me, Biddy –

Rachel exits. Nathaniel rejoins his bride. Biddy looks after Rachel, intently. In another part of the stage Alice starts to pack.

SCENE NINE

The wedding party continues on one part of the stage. Adam is saying his goodbyes – looking around for Rachel. At the same time Rachel enters her house, breathless, disturbed.

Rachel It's good we are going! We will be free of this place.

Alice is on the floor, sorting, packing. Rachel is suddenly struck with a thought.

Oh, but my children! I must say goodbye to my children!

She attracts her mother's attention.

I must bid farewell to my babies. I cannot leave this place without touching their names.

Alice *Go. Go. I will prepare everything.*

Rachel *I will not linger. Tell Adam I will be with him soon.*

Alice presses her daughter to her.

I love you, Mamma.

Rachel kisses her head. They hold each other for a moment and then Rachel exits. The wedding party disperses. Alice goes to the blanket-box to see what she must take from it. She starts to take out her sewing instruments. She roots around further. Adam enters. Alice does not hear him.

Adam Are we ready? Where is Rachel?

Suddenly Alice pulls Nathaniel's military jacket from the bottom of the box. She sees Adam. They both stare at the jacket. She looks in the pockets. Alice pulls out the knife. Alice holds it up. She looks at Adam.

It belongs to the boy, doesn't it?

Pause.

He has lied in everything.

He holds out his hand for the knife.

Give it to me.

She shakes her head. Adam goes and snatches the knife from her and puts it in his belt. Alice is worried. She goes to him and tries to take the knife back off him. He shakes her off.

(*Angry.*) Leave me be, Alice. I need it!

SCENE TEN

Adam storms off. Alice gathers up their few belongings as Rachel enters the place of stones. Rachel kneels before the three small stones. Her children's graves. She signs her old sign for 'Nathaniel' – reclaiming the name. She touches each stone. Alice exits as Biddy enters.

Biddy I am not a literate woman, Rachel. I know you think me stupid. But I can read signs. Did you know that, Friend? Not the signs of the deaf and the dumb. The signs that a man and a woman make with their bodies.

Rachel looks at her a moment.

Rachel I must go home, Biddy. Adam is waiting for me.

Biddy Poor Adam. The truest man among us. It is not right what you have done.

Rachel looks at her again.

You were more than a mother to the boy, were you not?

Rachel What I did was wrong.

Biddy You do not even deny it! You must have all the men – you are nothing but a whore –

Rachel Biddy – you do not understand –

Biddy Oh, I do understand. You think me stupid but I understand everything! I understand that I was clear to marry Adam. I was clear and he was clear. We were promised to one another. And then you came.

Rachel (*shocked*) I did not know it was so advanced – Adam did not tell me –

Biddy He gave me his word. And then he set me down. I could tell you the promises he spake – would you hear them? I have them by heart, Rachel.

Rachel Biddy – I am sorry. I am so sorry! But these sorrows are long passed.

Biddy They are not passed! They are with me every day! Do you know how hard it was for me to love you, Rachel? But I did it because of my faith. I made you my friend – my best friend.

Rachel And I thank you for your love –

Biddy I cannot love you any more –

Rachel Biddy! You do not need to suffer any more. We are going – Adam and I – we are leaving today –

Biddy Adam cannot leave! Adam is ours. Adam belongs to us.

Rachel But – Adam wants to go.

Biddy No! It is you who must go. You do us harm. You do my children harm.

Rachel No indeed –

Biddy My Tabitha did eclipse you. Nathaniel chose her over you. And yet you would still have him. When you have Adam! You have Adam! –

Rachel It is not true – I do not want him –

Biddy You tried to do the same thing to her that you did to me!

Rachel No –

Biddy You are nothing. You do not know what it is to be a mother. To want what is best for your children – it is a force – greater even than the love of God –

She takes up a stone and throws it at Rachel.

Rachel Friend Biddy –

Biddy I am not your Friend.

Rachel Please – I will not fight you –

Biddy takes up another stone and strikes her with it.

Biddy! Wait . . .

Biddy picks up a large stone and advances on her.

Biddy Why will you not be silent?

Rachel I will not fight you.

Biddy When will you cease this endless talking!

Rachel stumbles backwards. Falls to the ground.

Rachel But I do not want to die. I want to live – please Biddy – I WANT TO LIVE!

Rachel curls herself into a foetal position as Biddy
stands over her and takes a huge swing with her rock.

Biddy I want you to be quiet!

She hits her hard on the head.
  Blackout.

SCENE ELEVEN

Adam and Rachel's house.
  Darkness. Adam enters. Rickman follows him.
Perhaps they hold lanterns.

Rickman The light is gone for today, Adam! There is no
use searching any more. We will start again at first light.

Alice enters. Goes to Adam. Urgent.

Alice *Where is she? Where is my daughter? Have you*
found her?

She prods his chest. Urgent. Adam holds her away
from him. Shaking his head. Not looking at her
directly.

Adam We did not find her. I'm sorry.

Alice starts to pace. Wringing her hands. In pain. The
men look at her.

Rickman Poor creature. It is difficult to know how to
comfort her.

They watch as she goes and kneels by the blanket-box.
Rachel's former cot. Suddenly there is a knock at the
door. Adam and Rickman look at each other. Adam
goes. Alice looks up. Hope? Tabitha enters with
Nathaniel. Followed by Biddy.

84

Biddy We could not sleep for worry. What word of dear Rachel?

Rickman shakes his head.

Rickman We will set out again in the morning. We will find her.

Biddy Oh Adam. I am so sorry for your troubles. But she will be back. In all likelihood she took it into her head to walk. Rachel has a yearning for the wild – you called her a disorderly walker – did you not, James? But God will keep her safe. She will be sheltered under a bush most like. Sleeping sounder than we are sleeping!

Rickman (*be quiet*) Bedelia –

Nathaniel You should look for her in the town. I will go with you. I know where she sometimes walks.

Adam stares at Nathaniel. Alice is watching Biddy. She becomes the silent witness of the rest of them during this scene.

Biddy Yes! She loves the town. She has friends in the town. More's the pity. You are right, Nathaniel! That is where she must be gone. But she will be back tomorrow! I know it! She would not desert you, Adam. And her poor mother. Why, Good Alice is nothing without Rachel to speak for her. She would not abandon her –

Rickman Bedelia! There is no profit in this conjecture –

Biddy (*bruised*) I am sure I am only trying to help –

Rickman We achieve nothing with this. We should all go home. We should get some rest.

Adam (*deadly*) No. There will be no rest tonight.

He looks at Nathaniel.

What say you, Friend?

Adam goes up to Nathaniel.

Where is my wife?

Nathaniel Why do you ask me?

Tabitha Adam, why do you speak so strange?

Adam (*to Nathaniel*) WHERE IS SHE?

Rickman Adam, what is this?

Nathaniel (*overlapping*) I know not!

Adam (*to Nathaniel*) What have you done to her? Where is she? Lead me to her.

Nathaniel I swear I do not know where she is.

Adam pins Nathaniel against a wall.

Adam You lie to me! You lie to us all. You lie and you lie and you lie!

Tabitha Pappa – make him stop!

Adam Tell them who you really are. Tell your wife. Go on.

He pushes him before Tabitha. Biddy shields her daughter.

Biddy You are scaring us, Adam.

Adam Or shall I tell her?

Rickman Adam, what is this?

Adam This man is no Quaker.

Biddy I am sure you are mistaken –

Adam He is a soldier. A fighter. Everything he has said about himself is untrue. His background. The letters of commendation. Everything is fake.

The others are staring at Nathaniel.

Rickman Nathaniel?

Nathaniel I fought. It is true. But I deserted – I told them my conscience objects –

Rickman turns to Adam.

Rickman If this is true – if he rejects the military – then perhaps it is our duty to be his refuge –

Adam He deserves no refuge! He seduced my wife!

Tabitha What?

Nathaniel No. No. It was she who seduced me!

Tabitha starts to cry.

Biddy Oh my Tabby.

Nathaniel It was before we were married, Tabitha – she means nothing to me –

Adam shoves Nathaniel.

Adam Where is she? What have you done with her? What have you done with my wife?

Nathaniel I have not touched her!

Adam Did you kill her?

Nathaniel You have lost your mind –

Adam I know what happened! She rejected you. She stood up to you and so you killed her. Is it not so?

Nathaniel laughs.

Rickman Adam – what are these wild imaginings?

Biddy Perhaps Adam speaks true. We do not know what this boy is capable of.

Tabitha Mother! How can you say that?

Adam (*to Nathaniel*) You will leave this place. Your presence is poison.

Nathaniel I have a right to be here. I am married to one of yours –

Adam As of now your union is undone!

Tabitha No!

Nathaniel But Adam, I think you know the truth about Rachel. The plain truth. Listen to your heart. Your wife is not dead, is she? She has deserted you. You weren't man enough for her.

Adam takes out the knife, hurls himself at Nathaniel and pins him to the ground.

Rickman Adam!

Adam stares at Nathaniel.

Adam I know what you are. You are WORTHLESS! LOVELESS! GODLESS!

He indicates Nathaniel's heart and forehead.

I will carve it here and here so all the world can read it.

Rickman In God's name, man, give me the knife –

Nathaniel You will kill me, will you? Quaker that you are?

Rickman Do not let him come between you and your testimonies, Adam. ADAM!

Nathaniel I admit that I lied. I have always lied. I came from nothing. I lie in order to survive. But this one thing is true: I looked up to you, Adam. I loved you best of all.

Adam (*with difficulty*) I do not want your love.

Gently Rickman takes the knife from Adam. Adam gets up and walks away. Nathaniel gets up during the next. Dusts himself off.

Nathaniel No! No! My love isn't good enough for you, is it?! You know what? You are liars – all of you. You speak Friend this and Friend that but you do not love each other. You do not live in communion. You live in proximity. You hide yourselves away from the dirt, the noise and the guts of life because you are frightened of living. You and your conscience amounts to nothing. History is on the side of the men with the guns!

Biddy This man is dangerous! We need to inform the militia. They will bring him to justice.

Tabitha Mother!

Nathaniel Then I will be hanged for desertion. I will die. You may as well kill me now.

Tabitha (*crying*) No!

Nathaniel Will you kill me, Adam? Come. Do your worst.

Adam stares at him. Considers it. Then looks away.

Adam (*quietly*) He must leave this place.

Nathaniel Oh, I will go. But you should know this: I did not kill your wife.

Biddy How can we believe him?

Nathaniel I am not in the habit of killing women.

Tabitha You see!

Rickman We cannot decide this now. We need to sit – we need to be calm –

Tabitha If he says he did not kill her, he did not. I believe him.

Biddy Oh child.

Tabitha I love him.

Biddy No, you do not.

Tabitha You made me love him. Both of you. You invited him in!

Rickman We were misled –

Tabitha I do not care what he has done. I forgive him.

Biddy How can you say that?

Tabitha Is that not the basis of our faith? Is that not our practice? That is what you have taught me.

They all look at her.

Rickman The child is right.

Pause.

Perhaps we must find a way to reconcile him to our hearts.

Biddy But how can we ever trust him?

Nathaniel I – I – want a life here –

Tabitha You see!

Nathaniel I can be different – I can be like you – please give me that chance –

Adam But what of my wife?

Biddy I'm sorry to say it, Adam, but Rachel always wanted the town.

Adam Does that mean she deserved to die?!

Biddy We do not know if she is dead.

Rickman Pray God she is alive.

Tabitha Perhaps she meant to lose herself!

Adam What?

Tabitha Perhaps she does not want to be found.

Pause. Tabitha goes to Adam. Takes his hands.

Adam. You have always loved me as if I were your own,
I know that.

He looks at her.

If you want me to be happy, then you will let me have
Nathaniel. You were the first to wish us blessings in our
married life. Do you remember, Adam?

Pause.

We can search for Rachel at first light. If she wants to be
found – why then we will find her! But it is late now and
I am tired. I am going home now – with my husband.

Adam looks at Nathaniel.

Come, Nathaniel.

*Nathaniel looks at them all and then leaves with her.
They do not stop him. Pause.*

Rickman Shall we sit? Shall we pray?

Biddy I cannot pray –

Rickman It is right to pause. Offer it up to God.

*Adam nods absently at him. The men sit. Biddy
remains standing. She becomes aware of Alice staring
at her.*

Bedelia!

*Biddy sits. She tries to bow her head. She is in an
extreme state of distress. Alice is still staring at her.
Biddy looks up. Looks down again quickly. Slowly*

Alice comes up to her. Biddy is scared. Alice is now pointing at her.

Alice *Where is my daughter? Where is Rachel?*

Biddy is shaking her head.

Biddy (*quietly*) No.

Alice *You know where she is. You know.*

Biddy puts her hands over her ears.

Take me to where she is.

Biddy starts to cry.

Biddy I am so sorry, Alice.

The men look up and stare at her. Alice looks at Adam and points to Biddy. Biddy looks at Adam.

I did not mean to hurt her.

Adam Biddy?

Biddy Oh Adam. How can you forgive me?

Rickman What have you done?

Biddy I am afraid to tell you –

Rickman (*gently*) Biddy – we need to find Rachel –

Biddy I – I hit her –

Rickman What?

Biddy She did try to usurp my child. Like she usurped me.

Adam shakes his head.

Adam Where is she?

Biddy I don't know.

Rickman You must know.

Adam Is she dead? For God's sake, woman, tell me!

Biddy (*scared*) No, believe me when I left her, she was breathing.

Adam stands.

She was at her children's graves.

Adam But we searched there!

Biddy But that's it, you see. She is not there any more.

Adam What?

Biddy I returned to her, Adam. I did. I felt such remorse. I wanted to help her. But she was gone.

Rickman stands.

Rickman Take us there.

They exit.

SCENE TWELVE

The place of stones. Darkness. Biddy leads them breathlessly to the place where she and Rachel fought. Adam kneels. Touches the ground.

Biddy You see! She is gone! I did not lie.

Adam There is blood.

Biddy We fought. But she was not dead. She must have left of her own free will.

Rickman We will go to the town tomorrow. We will enlist help. We will find her.

Pause.

Biddy I am sorry, Adam.

Adam Why would you do this to me?

Pause.

Biddy (*quietly*) I was clear for you, Adam. Forsaking all others.

Pause.

Adam You are deluded.

Pause.

Biddy Take me to the town. I will hand myself over to the authorities.

Rickman We are the Religious Society of Friends! What will they think of us?

Biddy turns to Rickman.

Biddy You must say goodbye to the children for me, James. Forgive me but I cannot bear to do it myself. Tell them that I love them . . . You will raise them so well. You are the best father to them.

Rickman Biddy –

A shared moment between Rickman and Biddy.

Adam No! No town. No militia. God is our judge.

Biddy No, I want to be punished. It is only right.

Pause.

Adam Go home, Biddy. The baby will be calling for you.

She stares at him.

Biddy You will forgive me? I cannot live without your forgiveness –

Adam (*sharply*) GO HOME!

She nods, upset. She leaves. Stumbling out.
  Pause.

Rickman (*grateful*) Adam –

Adam Go with her! It is not safe.

Rickman (*at a loss*) Our community is broken! Oh, Adam! I am so tired of eldering. Who are we now? What are we to become?

Adam I do not know.

Rickman Adam, you must be elder in my place –

Adam See to your wife.

  Pause. Rickman nods at Adam and leaves. Adam and Alice are left. Alice goes to the gravestones. Kneels there. Adam joins her.

You know everything, don't you, Alice?

  Pause.

Rachel is alive. But she is gone from us . . . It is true. I was not enough for her.

  He starts to cry. Alice comforts him. He looks at her.

It is just us now.

  They stare at each other. Adam takes her hands in his. Looks at them. Looks at her. Touches his mouth as he speaks.

I will be your voice.

  She looks at him.

And you will be my hands.

  She nods.

SCENE THIRTEEN

Alice leaves. Adam gets up slowly and goes to the stone and starts to work away at it. Nathaniel joins him. He looks at Adam. Looks down. Shuffles a little, embarrassed.

Nathaniel Is there any word of Rachel?

Adam No word.

Pause.

Nathaniel My name is Robert Garson. My father did despise me, Adam. I knew nothing but his anger from an early age –

Adam puts his hand up to him to stop.

Adam It matters not where you came from. Only where you are going

Nathaniel No. I want you to know who I really am. My name is Robert Garson –

Adam You are Nathaniel to me.

Pause.

Nathaniel (*vulnerable*) Tabitha is with child. I am going to be a father. I need you to teach me how to be, Adam.

Adam looks at him and then indicates that he should join him in work.

Adam Work with me.

Adam starts to work. Pauses.

I was an apprentice too, you know. My master set me to building walls. And he taught me that every stone has its place. It is up to us to find it.

*Adam works on. Nathaniel hangs back. Adam looks
at him.*

You want to be my apprentice – so work with me. We
will work beside each other till – please God – I can
restore you to my heart. It will take time. Till we can be
restored to each other. Till all is restored.

*Nathaniel joins him. They keep a respectful distance
from one another*

Nathaniel Thank you.

*Music. The restoration of the Meeting. A choreo-
graphed sequence. The men work. At the same time
the women work. Then they meet for worship. They
sit. They shake hands. The men work. The women
work. Alice fits Tabitha with a maternity dress. They
meet for worship. They sit. They shake hands. Alice
teaches Adam to sign.*

Alice *In the beginning was the Word –*

*He copies her signs. The men work. The women work.
They meet for worship. They sit. They shake hands.
Alice teaches Adam again.*

And the Word was with God. And the Word was God.

*He signs back to her more confidently. Two, three
times. Alice is satisfied and leaves. The men stay. Work
again. Slowly during this the light starts to dawn.*
    *Nathaniel works on as Alice re-enters holding a
letter, with haste, with joy. She shows it to Adam.*

Adam A letter?!

She gives it to him.

It is from Rachel.

*She nods. Nathaniel looks at Adam respectfully and
then leaves. In another part of the stage Rachel enters.*

She has been walking for a long time. She looks older, more ragged, but calm. He opens the letter and tries to read. His eyes swim with tears.

I can't read it – the letters fly about –

Alice takes it from him. She looks at it.

Read it to me, Alice.

He holds it up to her. Rachel speaks the words as Alice signs them. Adam watches Alice's hands.

Rachel / Alice *Adam. Know that I am alive. And I am well. Do not blame Biddy for her actions. I had wanted to die so badly – but in that moment she taught me that I had no choice but to live . . . My first thought was to return to you. But I had an even greater leading inside me. I knew I had to walk straight into the battlefield. For the world, you know, is a battlefield. Oh but it is beautiful too, Adam. I have found kindness and sanctuary wherever I go. I know now that human beings can be brave, generous, strong – even in the most difficult circumstances . . . And as for me, I am finding my voice in the world. I minister wherever I go. Not all will hear me. But that is not my concern. At last I am finding my power. I am finding my truth, the truth that was always inside me . . .*

Alice takes the letter and reads the next part to herself. Adam sits and watches Alice. Rachel speaks.

Rachel Tell Mamma that the red ribbon is still around my wrist. It has stretched longer than I ever thought possible. I hope she feels it too.

Alice smiles.

Tell her that my hands still speak to her. Every night. They fly of their own accord – like little birds sending messages to her across the sky.

Alice goes to the blanket-box. They watch her as she opens the box and takes a fragment of red ribbon out of it. She ties it around her wrist. She sits.
Rachel turns to Adam.

Know above all, my beloved Adam, that my heart still beats in tune with yours. If you are very quiet, then you will hear it. Close your eyes and I am still with you. Your Rachel.

He closes his eyes. She leaves.
At the same time as Rachel leaves, Biddy and Tabitha enter. Tabitha is holding her baby, a new bundle of linen. Biddy gently pushes Tabitha forward.

Tabitha Adam?

He opens his eyes and sees the baby.

He is born. My son. Will you hold him?

He shakes his head, nervous. Tabitha smiles and thrusts the bundle in his arms. It has a huge effect on him. He softens. Curls in to the child.

Adam A boy?

Biddy Tabitha and Nathaniel have chosen a name for him.

Tabitha We would call him Adam!

He looks at her. Says nothing.

But only if it please you?

He says nothing. Looks at the baby.

Adam (*emotional*) He is lovely.

He hands the baby back to Tabitha. She smiles.

Tabitha He is, isn't he! He is such a good boy.

Adam Yes. We are all born in goodness.

The two women look at him and then go to exit.
Biddy turns.

Biddy You are coming to Meeting, aren't you? Adam?

He says nothing. Alice gets up and is the first to go and
sit for Meeting. The Meeting starts to assemble around
her.
Adam stands adrift in the middle of the space.
The whole community sits. They all wait for Adam.
He looks at them all. Finally he sits.
Silence.
Alice's head is bowed. She is in a deep internal place.
Suddenly she makes a noise. A strangled noise in her
throat.

Alice AR – GH –

A few look at her. Some keep their heads purposefully
down. Embarrassed. Adam looks at her, then looks
down again.

ARGH – WUR –

Adam looks at her. More curious.

Adam Alice?

The spirit is rising in her.

Alice AHH WANN – TUR –

The others stare in astonishment at Alice.

SPUKKKK.

She is propelled to standing.

Tabitha What is she doing?

Biddy Does she ail? Adam? What is wrong with her?

Adam (*in wonderment, realising*) No. She doesn't ail.

There is agitation in the Meeting.

Don't you see the Spirit moves her?!

Alice I WANN TER SPIK!

Rickman Good Heavens! What is the right ordering for this?

Adam There is no right ordering for this.

Alice I WANTASPEEK.

Biddy There must be an advice for this!

Adam We need no advice.

There is a murmur of disquiet, fear around the Meeting. 'Can she speak?' 'What if we don't understand her?' 'I didn't know she could speak!'
Alice steps forward and speaks slowly, with great difficulty. They go silent. Each word costs her emotionally and physically.

Alice (*speaks*) I HEAR – GOD. SHE SPEAKS TO ME . . . IN MY MAMMA'S VOICE. But no! I don't want God. I HATE GOD! I tell her: DAUGHTER GONE. I WANT TO DIE! . . . But God says no. NO DIE. YOU LIVE! YOU STRONG! . . . DEAF STRONG! . . . My daughter – gone. My daughter – walk.

Rachel enters. She weaves in and out of them as they sit. They do not see her. Only Alice sees her. She looks at her daughter with love.
Rachel reaches Alice. The two women look at each other. Intense.

Rachel *I hold you in the light, Mamma.*

Alice *I hold you in the light, daughter.*
I love daughter. I say: GO: DAUGHTER. WALK!

Rachel nods at her and exits. Alice watches her go.
Lets her go. Then she turns to the others.

Now! We sit . . . TOGETHER. WE HURT! PAIN
together. DARK together . . . But we look – to the light.
WE ARE THE LIGHT! WE ARE LIGHT!

She is shaking. After a moment she sits. The silence
intensifies. Adam stands.

Adam Alice is truly our witness. She holds all the
wisdom of our Meeting – and all our weakness too. She
teaches us how powerful the silence can be. But without
her voice we are nothing. We are not Friends. We are not
community. We are no society . . . We must look to Alice
now. We must listen to her. For it is she who is our elder.

Adam looks at Alice.

Alice! Elder.

I hold you in the light.

She smiles. Stands. Signs back.

Alice *I hold you in the light.*

Slowly Biddy stands too and signs too, to Alice –

Biddy Elder –

I hold you –

She looks to Adam who teaches her the sign.

Adam *In the light.*

Biddy *I hold you in the light.*

Nathaniel stands.

Nathaniel *I hold you in the light.*

Rickman stands.

Rickman *I hold you in the light.*

Tabitha stands, overlaps with them.

Tabitha *I hold you in the light.*

They have all heard her. The whole community. They are all standing now – they keep speaking. They sign to each other. 'I hold you in the light.' Over and over again. A dance of hands. Birds flying. A whoosh of air and energy and light. Lights fade.

The End.